# UNLOCKING THE
# ENTERPRISER
# INS!DE

A Book of
Why, What
and How!

# UNLOCKING THE
# ENTERPRISER
# INS!DE
A Book of
Why, What
and How!

## Shailendra Vyakarnam
University of Cambridge, UK

## Neal Hartman
MIT Sloan School of Management, USA

 **World Scientific**

NEW JERSEY · LONDON · SINGAPORE · BEIJING · SHANGHAI · HONG KONG · TAIPEI · CHENNAI

# Contents

# Acknowledgements

We cannot have written this book without the long cast of supporters, enthusiasts, sponsors and most of all the Enterprisers. We would especially like to acknowledge the Cambridge MIT Institute (CMI) that had been formed to instil a culture of entrepreneurship and competitiveness in the UK economy. CMI identified and helped to transfer a course called Leadershape from MIT to Cambridge. In the journey across the Atlantic, which started with numerous colleagues from within Cambridge and other Universities, the programme gradually transitioned into one that focused on enterprise skills. The journey really took root with Anthony Ives, followed by Andrew Mitchell and more recently Orsi Ihasz and Gill Ellis. We also owe a great debt to the enterprise team from University of Sussex (Sally Wright, Sally Atkinson and Sharon Phillips) University of Newcastle (Gareth Trainer and his team), the Scottish Institute of Enterprise (Sharon Bamford) all of whom gave us critical mass and early trust to develop our experiments.

Enterprisers requires numerous facilitators to make it all happen and we are hugely grateful to about 200 of them, all of whom have given of their time, motivation, energy and practical insights to help make the programme happen. A few of them have come repeatedly, sponsored individuals to attend and lobbied and cajoled sponsors on our behalf. To them we owe that extra hug! This is a really difficult paragraph because we are sure to end up excluding someone we did not mean to, but here are the people we should really acknowledge; Prof Max Robinson, Kate Partridge, Katie Hart, Christopher Poczka, Jonathan Markwell, Vicky Mountford, Sunny Kotecha, Linda Florio,

Adam Moore, Mark Delamere, Richard Sant, Tony Greenwood, Lizzie Brown, David Owen, Claire Adamson, Simon Brookes, Nicola Andrews, Jessica Williamson, Georgina Voss, Nicki Lehrer, Bonnie McKenzie, Becky Miller, Simon Stockley and Simon Pratten. We did not push them to help us with the book, but their interventions, advice and feedback has helped us to shape it and to keep us focused on getting it written so that we may inspire others to take up the task.

There have been particular inputs to shaping the programme and this has come through Dr Shima Barakat and Dr Joanna Mills. They have helped to develop certain components of Enterprisers and shape the nature of the book. We would also like to thank Nicky Reynolds who helped edit and re-edit the book with a great deal of patience.

With all this help and generosity of spirit we have developed what we think is a book that is a bit different in the enterprise education field. In the end though while we give credit to our friends and allies, we take all the blame for anything that is not quite right in the book!

# Chapter 1

# Entrepreneurship is Becoming a Social Movement

We see enterprise and entrepreneurship increasingly becoming a social movement in most of the world — it is neither the preserve of a few odd people nor a fashion accessory of politicians. We need go back only 50 years to see the very dramatic changes that have taken place in society, where[1] structural changes in society have caused a greater degree of individualisation, resulting in people having to flexibly restructure their resources, codes of behaviour and ethics, eventually making their own work/life choices and thus shaping their own destinies.

> I forced myself to think what the new concept is and it became clear to me that it was risk, not only in technology and ecology, but in life and employment, too. From Ulrich Beck — www.brainyquotes.com —

This book is meant for policy makers, educators, business advisors who work for government agencies, investors and bankers. The book is also likely to be of help to consultants who work with entrepreneurs. Of course we welcome other readers and hope you too can take something from this book!

This opening chapter outlines the big social changes that are taking place as a way of setting the context for enterprise development. We see that these big changes are causing people to re-think the way they see their own futures, the contribution they can make and therefore the rewards they can expect. From the macro view of why we think entrepreneurship development is important we take a look at the more personal reasons that people have, their contexts and how we can better understand these in order to support enterprise development.

In Chapter 2 we provide a helicopter view of the literature that covers entrepreneurship and the key frameworks that have shaped entrepreneurship education. These frameworks have evolved over time and are rooted in management education. As knowledge in the area develops there are increasing doubts about basing entrepreneurship education on management principles, especially when entrepreneurial learning itself is thought to be a slippery concept. In Chapter 3 we set out the historical context of entrepreneurial education and describe some of the tools and techniques currently used in this form of education. We also ring an alarm bell for educators. Media, especially TV and private sector web based organisations is gaining rapid influence by creating programmes and content that inform and inspire. It will not take long before these forms of media are able to replace what is currently offered by educators.

In Chapter 4 we set out the portfolio of courses that have been developed in Cambridge at the Centre for Entrepreneurial Learning — sharing what we have done and what more needs to be done to develop "education for entrepreneurship". The reason for providing this insight is that we want to set the context of Enterprisers — which has a very particular place in the learning journey of those who participate. In addition to separating out the Education about and the education for curricula, we will also argue that education that raises levels of risk tolerance is a necessary part of enterprise education. In Chapter 5 we start to describe the unique collaboration between University of Cambridge and Massachusetts Institute of Technology (CMI) that lead to an experiment with a new form of enterprise programme. We brought together communities of undergraduates from Cambridge, MIT and over 65 other Universities over several years and programmes. We experimented with a variety of models and made changes as we went along so that by the 10th version we had established a totally unique enterprise experience for groups of people. We believe this is the first time that there has been an educational course developed in this revolutionary way, included so many people as participants and pioneered enterprise education that combines creativity, opportunity recognition and business know-how — all at high speed. The outcomes have been significant and inspirational and we base many of our arguments on the "how to teach entrepreneurship" on the basis of what we have learnt while developing Enterprisers. This chapter deals with the vision and structure of this form of enterprise education.

Chapter 6 deals with a very particular question! We often get asked if one can teach entrepreneurship. Well here is our question — who is best equipped to help teach it? What skills do they need and what sort of people should they be? We try and set out the characteristics of the facilitators of learning and enablers of enterprise teaching. This may seem anecdotal and particular to Enterprisers. We make no apology for this because it is the first time that thought has been given to this question. In the main we ask about the characteristics of entrepreneurs and ask what they need to know and learn and do, but we rarely ask who should teach it and what they need to be like. In Chapter 7 we ask — how to measure all this activity? In parallel with this study scholars have been collecting data on a longitudinal basis about the raised levels of self-efficacy. We draw on their reports in this chapter and also illustrate case studies of people who have made changes to what they do. There are both philosophical and practical questions about how one can measure the impact of enterprise education. We present some of these debates and draw our own conclusions of what can and should be measured.

Chapter 8 concludes with case histories of institutions and individuals who have used what they learnt. It also has vignettes of insight from people who have been inspired to act, even if they did not take the detail of the programme into their next steps. The authors conclude with their own Ah Ha moments.

The positioning of this book in the sphere of entrepreneurship education is probably best summed up by the Triple Helix (see Fig. 1.1 below) which describes the connections between know how, social skills and personal awareness to raise confidence, self belief and eventually entrepreneurial intent. These constructs of knowing how entrepreneurial behaviours are carried out, enabled by a learning by doing model, we think, raises a sense of self confidence because even small steps of action — even if they are simulated, provides a further step towards raised self belief — which is central to the issue of motivation to carry out an enterprising project.

The sum total of all this activity and personal development leads to the raising of entrepreneurial intent. This last construct of enterprising behaviour is the bedrock of being able to spot opportunities and immerse oneself in entrepreneurial ecosystems and networks. There are many excellent books and courses on how to establish ventures and what to do next, all of which presuppose that one has the intention, confidence, resources and know-how to become alert

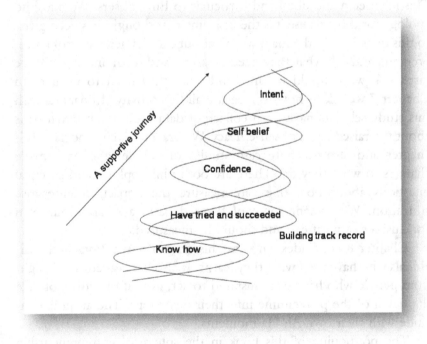

**Figure 1.1.**  Triple helix for developing entrepreneurial intent.

to opportunity and have the skills to seize them. We are focused on getting to the starting gate.

In designing the education needed to achieve this heightened state of intention, alertness and motivation, the learning objectives can seem diffuse and one of the interesting challenges in enterprise education which is a "contact sport", is that the learning needs to be facilitated and the process can come over as a series of "events" rather than as education and students sometimes find it hard to comprehend what is going on. We would use the metaphor of a jigsaw puzzle and that in essence as enterprise educators we need to provide all the pieces and some light touch guidance on how to assemble the final puzzle.

It is important that students and participants take ownership of learning and so the facilitators need to set the tone at the start of such a process and keep reminding students about the purpose and where they have reached in their learning journey.

Enterprise education often combines interactive learning activities and they need to be orchestrated in terms of "edutainment" — without losing sight of the overall purpose.

We hope you enjoy the book and get inspired by what you read to try out new things and gain in your own confidence to look at enterprise education in new and different ways.

But before we get deeply immersed in the education issues, let us look at the social imperatives for why this book is needed, why we need to think about education for entrepreneurship in new ways and how you can make the case to your peers, colleagues and others about the background need for this kind of work. These arguments are also compelling for students who are new to enterprise ideas.

## 1.1 Social Changes — The Driving Forces of Change

There have been significant political changes over the past 50 years that include the removal of the Berlin Wall, leading to the spread of the free market system across countries for the first time. We can also see evidence of these changes in the two largest countries, China and India. While China has adopted a free market system,

India is heading towards a liberal market, because the latter is clearer about its position viz a viz democratic systems to support its adoption of free markets. Not only are there big political changes, but there has been a very rapid shift in technology adoption everywhere, innovations that have disrupted market places, with products and even with ways people do business. In many cases, the barriers to entry are dropping rapidly and in some senses as a result of this there is also a democratisation of knowledge, not least through such organisations like Google.

### 1.1.1 *Free Markets and Democracy*

"Democratic capitalism[2]...involves changes in cultural precepts; hugely more efficient capital markets; increasing rates of technological development; enormous efficiencies in the application of technology; and, of the greatest importance, the expansion of human capital assets reflecting prior expansions of individual wealth; personal investment decisions relating to the acquisition of skills, education and experience; and, changing perceptions of work and leisure. This transformation in economic activity is best articulated in the United States. It would be a mistake, however, to believe its emergence is limited. As mentioned, recent policy and experience in the United Kingdom, Ireland, India and to a lesser extent China, suggest the dawning ubiquity of the phenomenon. In each case the resultant reality involves increased productivity, increased employment (although not necessarily job tenure), and stable prices. (p. 3 — Carl J. Schramm, 2006)

### 1.1.2 *The Business of Government is not Business*

Governments have become less inclined to believe that they can run enterprises. As we can see in the webpage below, over a twenty year period there has been a huge surge in enterprises "coming onto the market" and being to left to market forces. The move is from a supply

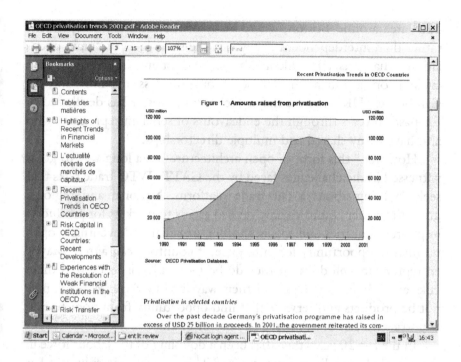

side mentality of the way markets work to a much more free market approach. At its peak, privatisation of state owned enterprises reached $100 billion. Although there has been a dramatic slowdown in privatisation, there is no doubt that it sowed a new way of thinking about business, not only in terms of ownership and governance, but also in terms of what behaviours were required from management in order to run their organisations in ways that were enterprising, sustainable and therefore becoming independent of state control and funding. More recently, although privatisation has slowed down, the new principles have started to percolate into management practice and one sees a surge in social enterprises as a way of dealing with services that sit between private good and social welfare.

### 1.1.3 *Brain Circulation*

Regional and global trade patterns are changing. For example it is argued that the more open and collaborative ways of working in Silicon Valley has allowed it to grow much faster than even the Route

128[3] area around Boston, where many of the firms are independent rather than interdependent. They lack the same level of "brain circulation" that exists in Silicon Valley. This brain circulation is also evident on a much smaller scale but no less dynamic way in Cambridge (UK) where a major technology cluster has developed in the past 40 years through the endeavours of serial entrepreneurs who also have many shared and multiple directorships.[4]

However,[5] this form of open architecture has a long way to go as witnessed in the challenges faced by the GATT/WTO trade talks that seek to bring about a fair trade platform. National and regional groups in richer countries have denied access to markets for producers in poorer countries and this is another area that will eventually open up further opportunity for enterprise, if countries can agree! Maybe entrepreneurs will do what they do best — which is to by-pass these talks and agreements and find their way into markets. While it may not be products and services that find opportunity from poor to rich countries we can certainly see the rise in migration.

In the last 20 years there has been a doubling of the labour force in the so-called capitalist market system.[6] This is such a big shift as it has placed nearly 2 billion people into a single labour market, where previously these populations existed in different economic and political systems. The result is that people not only have to understand the implications for labour laws, job creation, resource allocation and deeper construct of justice and fair-play, but individuals need to better understand what this means for their day to day existence and development.

The UN[7] predicts that some 2.3 million people will migrate each year from developing to developed countries in search of opportunity and this scale of migration carries with it a major challenge, not least on local economic systems, the environment and both the generation and distribution of wealth. Further it is predicted that some 600 million people are likely to be affected by rising sea levels and one must expect these people to move as well. The world recently coped with the seismic shift from socialism to democratic systems by adding to its workforce. Now we see that for economic, environmental and in some cases political reasons, people are on the move.

And, people are on the move for leisure as well. In 1995 there were 500 million on the move, by 2006 this had risen to 842 million per year (www.unwto.org) and this basically means people are absorbing new cultures, ways of doing things, seeing new opportunities and creating incomes around the world. …There are of course regional variations, with some parts of the world receiving more tourists than others, but on the whole these figures indicate rising wealth and the use of disposable income for leisure.

> As I write this chapter — in the study centre at Darwin College in Cambridge, there has been a continuous stream of bus loads of tourists being dropped outside about every 10–15 minutes, people who have come to Cambridge for sightseeing)

### 1.1.4  *Social Networks*

The rapid growth of social networks, exemplified in the work of Anna Lee Saxenian in California and the Y Myint and S Vyakarnam work in Cambridge demonstrates that boundaries are less easy to define, so creating new conditions of work that also require new responses. And, even as we write this book we see the explosive growth of "facebook; LinkedIn, MySpace" and innumerable other social networks that are creating new communities around the world".[8] These developments are creating global opportunities as never before and Generation Y[9] is reaching out to it because it looks fun and has stirred the imagination of possibilities among (mostly) young people. There has also been a greater move in western economies to embrace personal choice, freedom and autonomy in recent times[10] and this causes a fragmentation and atomisation of markets, jobs and opportunities. (see for example: www.pajamanation.com)

### 1.1.5  *Commercialising Knowledge*

There has been an increasing pace of technological change — the influence of science and the increasing role of Universities wishing to find ways of commercialising their knowledge base requires more people with wider and greater ability to transfer knowledge into the market.[11]

"Increasingly, large public and non-profit organizations are also turning to entrepreneurship in their efforts to become flexible and respond to pressures to "do more with less." Government rhetoric encourages universities in particular to become more entrepreneurial, increasing the commercialisation of research and contributing to economic growth. ... interviews with 40 faculty members ... suggest that risk taking is the most important dimension in developing an entrepreneurial university, and may be a prerequisite for commercialisation."[12]

### 1.1.6 *I am from Government — I am Here to Help*

In the UK, since about 2000, there has been a major shift towards the encouragement of graduate enterprise. For example, in March 2001 Sir Gareth Roberts was asked to review and make recommendations to strengthen the Government's approach to productivity and innovation. He reported back to the Government in 2002 and the emphasis on enterprise is clear.

An environment that encourages enterprise and supports people who take opportunities and risks is a crucial ingredient of productivity improvement. A strong entrepreneurial base is an essential driver of growth and prosperity in a modern economy. New and more dynamic businesses increase competitive pressures in markets and facilitate the introduction of new ideas, technologies and more efficient working practices.

Despite the rapid growth of the SME sector since the 1970's, rates of entrepreneurial activity in the UK remain moderate by international standards, in particular when compared to the US. To address this gap, the Government is taking steps to:

- establish and maintain a modern and competitive business tax system;
- reduce the regulatory burden on enterprise;
- address barriers to raising finance for small business;
- improve support for small and new business;
- promote a step change in the UK's enterprise culture.

One of the biggest studies of enterprise development that is starting to influence Governments to think more broadly about this topic is the Global Entrepreneurship Monitor, which seeks through large scale collaborative effort to report on the levels of enterprising activities at national and regional levels. Setting aside any scholarly misgivings on the research methodology or the accuracy of the findings, the trend lines are clear. More Governments, societies and individuals are getting engaged in enterprise and in the context of GEM — this means that more people are seeking self employment or to start businesses, in other words to become entrepreneurs.

As the world population increases, there is really only one country where the numbers of young people is big enough to support future older and retired people and that is India. For the rest of the world there is going to be a major shortage in the working population over the next 50 years, the result of which is going to be a growing pension's deficit and an urgent need for people to become self-reliant and have the assets and capability to take care of themselves in their twilight years. This demographic shift is accompanied — by and large — by the fact that in most places people are living longer and so need to have access to funds for longer periods. This sense of urgency is already hitting countries like the UK where pension's rules are shifting the burden of savings contributions from employers to employees.

Even in the mid 1970s the work of Schumacher in his book Small is Beautiful — highlighted in the key role of itinerant small businesses, and micro businesses as a route to self-reliance. His thesis was not based on the pension crisis, but rather on the need for self reliance because larger organisations were unlikely to provide freedom, autonomy for individuals and the sheer numbers of people involved in many countries meant that formal organisations did not have the absorption capacity to create the numbers of jobs needed. This is still a valid argument in many countries where unemployment and even under-employment are major problems.

Over the past 25 years or so, the implications of Small is Beautiful argument has lead to policies and interventions that stimulated small business and a small business mentality. In other words, it has lead to a kind of "replacement income enterprise". But while we can capture some of the spirit of enterprise in this — the key motivator is thought to be survival and is self-centred. It has become a way to remove unemployment and create localised incomes. These have seen huge successes, based, for example, on the work of people like Dr Yunus of Grameen Bank for example.

The downside has been the dead-hand of bureaucracy, projects that have created millions of people stranded in markets that are perfectly competitive (hairdressers, cabinet makers, itinerant workers of all kinds) who rely on Government employees, academics and consultants for their ideas, innovation and routes to market. We cannot afford to allow this kind of thinking and mistakes in the next generation of enterprise development.

In some ways we applaud the early work of McClelland and others who were focused on programmes of encouraging "achievement-Motivation" which have been long forgotten in favour of dry programmes of increased start-ups of SMEs. These have given rise to irrelevant statistics of the numbers of businesses rather than focusing on empowering people. But, it is clear that the growth of micro-finance, large scale government programmes and the work of large NGOS have focused on livelihoods and self employment.

And this means that people have to think about, learn skills and acquire a mind set of self reliance. Becoming more enterprising and mimicking the behaviours of entrepreneurs may be a solution. In reality this has begun in earnest over the past decade and we can see evidence of the surge in interest in entrepreneurship through a sampling of institutions, programmes and policy measures:

### 1.1.6.1 *The Evidence of a Growth in Enterprise*

Around every street corner — you can find networks, support, internet groups, policies from Government, incubators, bank programmes, business angel groups, business plan competitions, academics, University Departments, flag ship international awareness campaigns, Awards presentations, websites and much more.

Of course there are still parts of the world where entrepreneurship is very low on the social radar screens and where employment policies, regulations, tax regimes and political will is not yet geared towards individual freedoms and empowerment. Indeed in some areas there continue to be gender imbalances, lack of access to socially marginalised people and even certain corporate contexts can prevent people from being innovative and entrepreneurial. In order to raise the profile of enterprise education the World Economic Forum commissioned a report to highlight the gaps and provide cases and illustration of practise.[13]

The Global Entrepreneurship Monitor research program has been illustrating data from an increasing number of countries about the rates of entrepreneurial activity. It is increasingly ensuring that entrepreneurship is put in front of policy makers through league tables of countries and regions that have embraced entrepreneurship.[14]

A major influence for University based entrepreneurship derives from the Bayh-Dole Act which was enacted to "promote the utilization of inventions arising from federally supported research ... [and] to support the commercialization and public availability of inventions" This is a widely documented Act — the major effect of which has been to create a climate of transparency in technology transfer and is starting to encourage academics and University administrations to realize the economic value of their research.[15]

We have considered the big but not exhaustive list of macro reasons for enterprise development. It is sufficient to say that these macro forces on society have shaped our current thinking and looking to the future through the lens for example of the UN Millennium Goals or the forecasts of futurologists we can see, the need for people to be able to make their own choices become, being enterprising, innovative and be able to make things happen. Society, industry and Government and social enterprises need such people. Of course not everyone needs to be or can be an enterpriser — not because they do not have the genes — but because of a complex set of reasons that include personal motivations, circumstances, resources and opportunities.

But we take the view that everyone has an enterpriser inside and we should do what we can to help unlock this capability.

### 1.1.6.2 *Here is why an Entrepreneur Thinks it is Important*

We asked Dr Hermann Hauser, a hugely successful serial entrepreneur what he thought about the importance of entrepreneurship development.

> We asked Dr Hermann Hauser, a hugely successful serial entrepreneur what he thought about the importance of entrepreneurship development.
>
> Coming up with a business idea and then turning it into a major organization or even a modest self-sustaining business that supports the family is not easy.
>
> Having been involved in starting, supporting, mentoring, investing in and developing over 60 companies, many of which have had deep technology I know from both those firms that collapsed to those that made it big that entrepreneurship is truly important to an economy and also how hard it is to actually make it all happen.
>
> One of the merits of entrepreneurship education, in my experience, is that it can provide both the soft skills and the business know how to turn ideas into reality. Although creating ideas is more an intuitive process than a scientific one there is no question that being embedded in a social network with other students and nascent entrepreneurs is probably the best way to gain inspiration, motivation and resources to get

underway. Entrepreneurship education can help you by putting you into such networks and giving you the tools.

When I was starting my first company Acorn, in the late 1970s having completed my doctorate at Cambridge, the words entrepreneurship and business weren't in the university vocabulary! Since then we have managed to place these concepts at the heart of a big change in the University culture. One of the key stages in the change was the collaboration of the University of Cambridge with the Massachusetts Institute of Technology and it is really excellent to see the longer term outcomes of that collaboration.

### 1.1.7 *As One of My Family Elders Said "Even Educated People are Going into Business"*

Entrepreneurship comes in many forms, for example, when people bring the same set of skills, know how and drive as entrepreneurs for creating a social or civic change. Entrepreneurship is complex, takes time, is not fully understood and it is better to help people unlock their own capability and drive. Sadly there are ill-informed misconceptions like entrepreneurs are born, risk takers, lucky or rely on serendipity. None of these can be proved in a systematic way! And if one subscribes to them there is not much point in having an educational system!

Instead one needs to take a robust view of entrepreneurship development which focuses on five inter-related aspects:

(1) Raising awareness of inner motivation is the first step, because it can lead to
(2) Entrepreneurial intent, the consequence of which is that the sense of alertness to opportunity is heightened. This is tempered by a combination of
(3) Business skills and know-how — which are necessary conditions of success. This is balanced by

(4) Risk appetite which needs to be understood at an individual level and finally of course the entrepreneur needs an

(5) Opportunity which triggers a desire to succeed and outweighs the fear of failure. In combining all these so-called soft factors — we see individuals with a real sense of self-belief and confidence.

These qualities need an entrepreneurial ecosystem enabled by local social networks to provide for mentoring, investments, team members, legal and financial expertise and routes to clients and suppliers.

By instilling an enterprising capability, individuals are free to express this as employees or as individual forces of change. They take with them the energy, confidence, skills, knowledge and networks to make new things happen. People who are involved in making new things happen require a lot of resilience, persistence and abilities. And, for them to retain motivated through the early phases of entrepreneurship they need the fibre that provides strength.

In order to build these capabilities we have found at Cambridge that we need to build a portfolio of learning opportunities for students and we now summarize these as:

- Entrepreneurship education for the curious where students ask themselves what entrepreneurship is about, how it applies to them and where and how to look for support if they wish to start their journeys. (EE for curiosity)
- There is entrepreneurship education for those who want to "do it" but feel they would like reaffirmation, confirmation of their self-belief and develop a sharper intent and confidence. (EE for confidence)
- Opportunity recognition is one of the hardest elements of entrepreneurship and there is now a course run twice — for undergraduates and postgraduates that takes emerging technologies form the University and enables students to conduct a commercial feasibility study, thus learning how to balance the "hot" choice of a technology with "cold" market analysis. (EE to validate opportunities)
- Ignite is a one week deep immersion in a course that brings senior and experienced entrepreneurs to incubate novice and nascent

entrepreneurs. This means people who have decided to commercialise a technology whether it is from Universities, research institutions, from large corporations or their own ideas, the week helps to fast track the individuals and their ideas. (EE to make things happen)

- Most recently we have added an Advanced Diploma that combines much of what we have developed in the four programmes and pulled them together into a single opportunity for people to acquire a Diploma while working on their ventures. The signalling effect of the Diploma will hopefully be of value to the individuals as well as the learning that has been put in place.
- Video book to answer Frequently asked questions (FAQs)...............make EE more broadly accessible and available. See resources on www.cfel.jbs.cam.ac.uk

### 1.1.7.1 *Consider these Situations*

Graduates going to industry need to be better equipped with transferable skills, in addition to the knowledge they acquire in Universities. They need to have skills that are akin to enterprising people; such as; being creative with research and finding sources of funding, presentation of research and projects in ways that are accessible, practical implementation, negotiation and sales.[16] These qualities have a great overlap with people who want to start companies or charities. And how different would this be for people in civil service, University staff, health care and elsewhere?

We see increasing demands from companies to better understand entrepreneurship. There are law firms that describe themselves as entrepreneurial; large firms like Orange have senior manager labels as entrepreneurs, the term enterprising manager has become a root word in a large German firm. Companies like American Express; BT; Microsoft and others have sent their employees on entrepreneurship courses — to Cambridge University's Ignite programme. These firms are looking for innovation capacity rather than start-ups but they see many of the qualities and skills as common.

## 1.2 Enterprising Communities — The Next Stage of Enterprise Development

Because the "being an enterpriser[17] "is to be positive, seeking opportunities and making things happen — these aspirational goals are potentially uniting forces and this is where the agenda shifts from being restricted to making new things happen to enabling outward looking positive communities coming together — thus seeking to build enterprising communities.

We have exposure to this as an outcome of a programme called Enterprisers and we see its potential as a model to be applied to communities that are socially, economically deprived. We can see it as a model to find new forms of language to heal communities that have been torn apart by conflict. We have yet to prove this hypothesis, but in seeing the liberating energy amongst graduates we want to open up the discussion.

One of the reasons that this process of building enterprising communities can work — is that the model relies of bringing people who "have" with those that do "not have". It leverages the power of social capital and networks.

Bearing in mind people are constantly seeking to improve their condition, then enabling links for people to move upward/forward is a very powerful way to deal with enabling social change. Enterprisers as a model has this capability.

Going beyond a single example of a programme, the very purpose of building enterprising communities that seek new ways to improve their condition means that the concepts of enterprise and entrepreneurship become something far more powerful than "starting businesses".

Finally — there is a potentially curious additional role for entrepreneurship education — as a kind of Trojan horse for other disciplines. Take for example the teenage group getting ready for their final exams. How can we inspire or instil interest in subject areas like science and engineering when they might not see the connections between what they study and how their knowledge might be applied.

Enabling them to see these connections through role models of entrepreneurs and practical projects that draw on their knowledge for enterprising projects are potential mechanisms. We do not necessarily want a world full of entrepreneurs starting businesses or give the impression that this is a career of last resort, but if we can instil in young people a positive spirit, and skills to help make inspiring links they can apply these in other career choices — to consider making a difference as they grow.

Looking at it from the reverse side: lack of entrepreneurship and the associated innovation means that we remain locked in old systems, structures, and understandings.[18]

Through the outcomes of our work over the past five years with around 1,000 graduates we have come to see that both the spirit of enterprise or the character of being enterprising combined with an understanding of the processes of entrepreneurship — in our context the making of new things happen — can be a force for change in so many ways.

It is this insight, perhaps more modestly, this observation that has motivated us to write this book.

## Endnotes

1. U. Beck and M. Ritter (1992): Risk Society: Towards a New Modernity. Sage Publications. London (ISBN: 0-8039-8346-8)
2. Carl J. Schramm (2006) Making the Turn: Entrepreneurial Capitalism and Its European Promise Presented at the April 8, 2006 Meeting of the European Union Finance Ministers Vienna, Austria
3. Anna Lee Saxenian (1994) Regional Advantage. Harvard University Press.
4. Yin M. Myint, Shailendra Vyakarnam and Mary New (2005) The Effect of Social Capital in New Venture Creation: The Cambridge High-Technology Cluster. Journal of Strategic Change.
5. Bernard Hoekman (2002) Strengthening the Global Architecture for Development. The Post Doha Agenda. World Trade Review, 1; pp. 23–45.
6. Andrew Fabian and Martin Jones (ed): 2006. Conflict — Darwin College Lectures. Professor William Brown on Conflict and Labour, pp. 125–144.

7. United Nations Press Release Pop 952 (13th March 2007) *2006 Revision*, please contact Hania Zlotnik; Director, Population Division; New York, NY 10017, United States; Tel: 212 963 3179; Fax: 212 9632147.

8. Michael B. Arthur and Denise M. Rousseau (1996): The Boundaryless Career. A new employment principle for the new organisational era. Oxford University Press.

9. Generation Y is thought to follow Generation X — in that they are described as young, brash and informal in their work styles. However at present this probably best described as people in North America and other Anglo-phone regions. (see wikipedia for more immediate information.)

10. Charles Handy (1995) The Empty Raincoat. Making sense of the future. Random House.

11. See for example a number of reports such as the Lambert Review, the reports from the Higher Education Funding Council for England and the numerous business plan competitions run by Universities, all of which have web presence.

12. William T. Todorovic, Rod B. McNaughton, Paul D. Guild (2005): Making university departments more entrepreneurial: The perspective from within. International Journal of Entrepreneurship and Innovation. London: May 2005. Vol. 6, Iss. 2, pp. 115–122.

13. http://www.weforum.org/en/initiatives/gei/Entrepreneurship Education/index.htm

14. http://www.gemconsortium.org/

15. http://www.autm.net/aboutTT/aboutTT_bayhDoleAct.cfm

16. http://www.hmtreasury.gov.uk/consultations_and_legislation/lambert/consult_lambert_index.cfm

17. Need to insert reference to the text from David Rae re OED source.

18. (Yu, 2001 in Petrakis, 2005) Growth, Entrepreneurship, Structural Change, Time and Risk. P E Petrakis. Journal of American Academy of Business, Cambridge. Hollywood:Sep 2005. Vol. 7, Iss. 1, pp. 243–250 (8 pp).

# Chapter 2

---

# A Helicopter View of Entrepreneurship

We thought it would be helpful to draw on the major contributions to the field of entrepreneurship education and how it is presently understood. The texts we have selected are by no means exhaustive, but they probably represent the most influential thought pieces used by "teachers" everywhere when they develop courses in entrepreneurship. If you are familiar with it, you ought to skip past this section, but if you are not entirely familiar with it and are somewhat new to the field, you may well find it helpful.

We also review, briefly, the present understanding of entrepreneurship education in terms of what is covered, processes and some of the factors that influence the design and delivery of entrepreneurship education. We also cover some of the pedagogies that are used in entrepreneurship education, especially when it goes beyond business school curricula.[1]

## 2.1 So, What is the Heffalump?

We take a definitional perspective from economics because in the end this area of human endeavour relates to economic well-being. There are other definitions of entrepreneurs that may be taken from a more humanist, psychological perspective but for us, this is the soap box on which we stand!

The Oxford English Dictionary defines an entrepreneur as:

*'One who undertakes an enterprise; one who owns and manages a business; a person who takes the risk of profit or loss.'*

As far as the dictionary definition[1] is concerned, entrepreneurship is the act of being an entrepreneur. Entrepreneurship goes beyond start-up and management of a business. It can be equally applied to those working within a larger organisation. The definition proposed by Howard Stevenson at Harvard Business School perhaps describes much better what entrepreneurship is all about.[2]

*'Entrepreneurship is a management style that involves pursuing opportunity without regard to the resources currently controlled.'*

Howard Stevenson's definition includes:

• Pursuit of opportunity
• Rapid commitment and change
• Multi-stage decision making
• Using other peoples' resources
• Managing through networks and relationships
• Compensating for value created

## 2.2 A Bit of History — Economic Theories Underlying Entrepreneurship[3,4]

Economic theory is concerned with two major questions about society:

• How does a society create new wealth?
• How does a society distribute wealth among its members?

Wealth creation and distribution are absolutely fundamental to social progress. Entrepreneurship along with the development of innovative scientific ideas is a major mechanism for ensuring both wealth creation and distribution.

Entrepreneurship itself has been around for a very long time, and over the last 250 years three different theories have emerged.

### 2.2.1 *Classical Capitalist Economic Theory*

Adam Smith in 1776 described the capitalist as an owner-manager who combined basic resources into a successful industrial enterprise. Meanwhile, the French word "entrepreneur" (meaning to undertake) was introduced and used to identify the owner-manager of a new industrial enterprise.

### 2.2.2 *Neoclassical Theory*

The overall direction of these theories is that self interest ("the invisible hand") would guide individuals toward entrepreneurial behaviours. But towards the end of the 19th century, economic theorists saw no place for the entrepreneur. They argued that the market consists of many buyers and sellers who interact to ensure that supply equals demand. The market, which they described as a "perfect market" would therefore be at equilibrium, and this would be achieved by fluctuations in prices with supply levels. It followed that wealth would be created and distributed because of the way that this perfect market operates, and so did not allow for entrepreneurs to create new demand. This is considered to be mainstream economics and is most frequently taught in schools and universities. They defined perfect markets as:

- having many buyers and sellers, so no single one has an influence on the market price;
- prices are set by the operation of the market — by sales;
- products and services must all be equivalent in content so that they differ only in price;
- all buyers and sellers have complete knowledge of the market and the transactions that take place.

### 2.2.3 *The Austrian School*

In the early 20th century, Schumpeter[5] argued against neoclassical theory and insisted that entrepreneurship was far too important a part of capitalism to be ignored. He proposed that innovation or the use of an invention to create a new product or service was the driving force behind the creation of new demand for goods and services. The market was, therefore, not perfect but chaotic because of the regular occurrence of entrepreneurs entering the markets with new innovations. This process of "creative destruction" destroyed the static market described by the neoclassicists and created a dynamic market which had continuous changes in buyer and supplier behaviour. It was these entrepreneurs who developed innovations to create new demand that was the mechanism of wealth creation and distribution. Influenced by the Austrian School, a further contribution to entrepreneurship theory was made by Kirzner.[6] He defined entrepreneurs as individuals who grasp opportunities for pure entrepreneurial profit and that they did this by uncovering unnoticed profit opportunities by being alert to them.

## 2.3 The Entrepreneur as a Decision Maker

A further study in the early 20th century by Knight[7] considered entrepreneurship in relation to risk and uncertainty. He saw entrepreneurial gain as the reward for taking decisions under uncertain conditions and assuming responsibility for those decisions.

### 2.3.1 *Types of Entrepreneur?*

There are many different types of entrepreneurs; some of them are listed below:

- Nascent entrepreneurs — thinking about it;
- Novice entrepreneurs — first time out;
- Serial entrepreneurs — several businesses in sequence;
- Habitual entrepreneurs — several businesses in parallel;
- Entrepreneurial managers — characteristics of entrepreneurs but work for an employer.

But what are the common features of successful entrepreneurs? Extensive work has been done to try to pinpoint what the exact characteristics are and how their minds work. There is no set recipe but a number of studies have drawn together some of their key attributes, attitudes and behaviours.

## 2.3.2 Six Dimensions — Howard Stevenson

Howard Stevenson[8] looked closely at entrepreneurs both in start-up businesses and established companies, and developed a description of entrepreneurial behaviour based on six critical dimensions of business practice. At one extreme of each dimension, there is the entrepreneur who feels confident to seize an opportunity regardless of resource requirement and at the other, there is the manager whose aim is to utilise the resources they have as efficiently as possible. Figure 2.1 shows a representation of the six dimensions and their extremes.

Stevenson also suggested that entrepreneurs have a number of personal traits including:

- Tolerance for ambiguity
- Ability to create the illusion of stability
- Risk management

| Entrepreneur | Key business dimension | Manager |
| --- | --- | --- |
| Opportunity driven | Strategic orientation | Resource driven |
| Quick and short | Commitment to opportunity | Long and slow |
| Minimal with many stages | Commitment of resources | Complete in a single stage |
| Use or rent | Concept of control | Own or employ |
| Networks with little hierarchy | Management structure | Formalised hierarchy |
| Value-based and team based | Compensation and rewards | Individual and hierarchical |

**Figure 2.1**  Six dimensions of entrepreneurship – Howard Stevenson

- Attention to detail
- Endurance
- Long-time perspective

In summary, entrepreneurs identify opportunity, assemble the required resources, implement a practical action plan and harvest the rewards in a timely flexible way.

### 2.3.3 *The Entrepreneurial Mind — Jeffrey Timmons*

Jeffrey Timmons[9] found that successful entrepreneurs shared common attitudes and behaviours:

- Work hard and are driven by intense commitment and determined perseverance;
- Optimistic outlook;
- Strive for integrity;
- Burn with the competitive desire to excel and win;
- Dissatisfied with the status quo and seek opportunities to improve almost any situation;
- Use failure as a tool for learning;
- Eschew perfection in favour of effectiveness;
- Believe that they personally can make a difference.

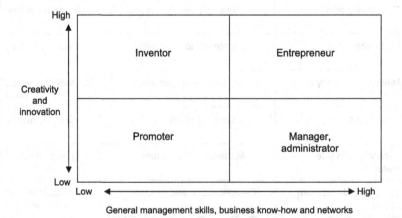

**Figure 2.2**   The relationship between creativity and management skills

In his view, entrepreneurs who succeed not only possess creative and innovative flair, but also have solid general management skills and behaviours.

### 2.3.4 The 10 D's — William Bygrave

William Bygrave[10] summarised the important characteristics of successful entrepreneurs in everyday words.

| | |
|---|---|
| Dream | Entrepreneurs have a vision and the ability to implement their dreams |
| Decisiveness | They make decisions swiftly, their swiftness is a key factor in their success |
| Doers | Once they decide on a course of action, they implement it as quickly as possible |
| Determination | They implement their ventures with total commitment |
| Dedication | They are totally dedicated and work tirelessly |
| Devotion | Entrepreneurs love what they do |
| Details | The entrepreneur must be on top of the critical details |
| Destiny | They want to be in charge of their own destiny |
| Dollars | Getting rich is not the prime motivator, but the measure of success |
| Distribute | Entrepreneurs distribute ownership of the business with key employees |

## 2.4 The Entrepreneurial Process

Shane and Venkataraman[11] set out a neat three-part summary of the entrepreneurial process, indicating opportunity discovery, venture creation and exploitation. They build on extant literature, and we have chosen to use the diagram given to us by Moore,[12] which has further detail for those of us who want to get more fine grained with teaching rather than with research.

The entrepreneurial process consists of three phases:

- *Innovation phase*: time when entrepreneurs generate and select ideas for new products or services.
- *Implementation phase*: a triggering event and the acquisition of capital and other resources.
- *Growth phase*: the success of the new venture and the need to acquire new managerial skills.

Each of these phases is influenced by a number of factors such as personal characteristics, the environment and the characteristics of the innovation as shown in Fig. 2.3.

A complimentary view is that the entrepreneurial process essentially brings together an opportunity an entrepreneur or entrepreneurial team and resources, and the forces behind the processes are that:

- It is opportunity driven;
- driven by a lead entrepreneur and an entrepreneurial team;
- it is resource thrifty and creative;
- it depends on the fit and balance among these and
- it is integrated and holistic.

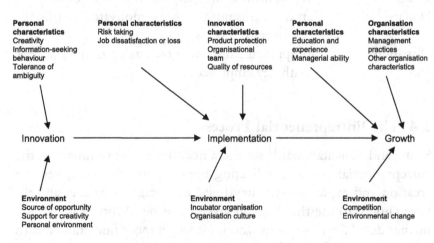

**Figure 2.3**   The entrepreneurial process

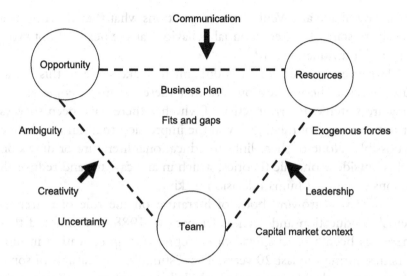

**Figure 2.4**   Timmons Model of the entrepreneurial process

At the heart of the process (depicted in Figure 2.4) is the opportunity. Not all ideas are opportunities, their recognition and evaluation is crucial but the important characteristics of good opportunities are that there is an underlying market demand for the product or service because of its value-added properties, and that it will generate money either as a profit or as a means of creating self-sufficiency for not-for-profit organisations.

Resources need to be understood and utilised wisely. For the entrepreneur, at the early stages they are scarce so the entrepreneur needs to minimise and control them as opposed to maximise and own. The entrepreneurial team is a key ingredient for success. A key element of resources that need to be understood are team members.

Meanwhile, the team requires determination and persistence, tolerance of risk, ambiguity and uncertainty, creativity, team focus of control, adaptability, opportunity obsession, leadership, communication. The tool which integrates the three together is the business plan.

There is extant academic work that covers definitions, characteristics, roles and responsibilities, actions and motivations of entrepreneurs. The substantive works are reviews of a mix of well-grounded empirical research and provocative reviews and reflections. The excellent review by Shane and Venkataraman positions what they describe as a transitory state of entrepreneurial behaviour at the nexus of opportunity and individual intent.[13]

However, as educators it is difficult to make sense of this literature, because the implications are that these are how people are — they are statements, irrespective of whether there have been surveys or not and none of them give you the impression that human change is possible. None of them links to educational literature or draws on fields outside economic theories, which in any case try and reduce all actions to rational human decision making.

There is a growing body of literature on the role of entrepreneurship education and even as far back as 1988, it was noted that there has been a rapid spread of entrepreneurship education in universities during the last 20 years. The distinguishing features of some of the newer degree programs included: (1) coverage of core basic area topics from the vantage point of start-ups, (2) knowledge pertaining to entrepreneurship in particular, (3) skill practice in persuasive communication in writing, oral presentation, and one-on-one negotiations, (4) more emphasis on creative thinking and synthesis, (5) authentic involvement in real-time ongoing entrepreneurship, (6) the creation of program venture plans by students, (7) practice in identification of opportunities stimulated around frontier technologies and path-breaking ideas and (8) exposure to role models of entrepreneurship.[14]

There is of course a growing body of literature from some of the newer scholars who are trying to understand how entrepreneurs learn to identify opportunities, grow into new roles and responsibilities and develop plans and actions to bring their ideas to life. However, in a systematic review of literature on entrepreneurship education, the picture painted was somewhat grim.[15]

## 2.6 It Is Like Cod Liver Oil — Good for You But We Don't Know Why!

There seems to be a lot of it but it is difficult to identify any sense of purpose or direction to much of it.

Among their various conclusions here is what they say:

> There is definitional and conceptual uncertainty and that outputs and outcomes are unmeasured in any consistent way so we do not yet know if any of it makes any difference!

There are several themes in research into entrepreneurship education that suggested the following areas of interest and concern:

- The policy climate for entrepreneurship education;
- The university context and enterprise climate;
- A series of activities that lead to pedagogical development within and outside the curriculum, increasing students' orientation and propensity for entrepreneurial careers;
- Academic enterprise and outreach activity predicated on the supply of faculty capability;
- Business/university interaction through consulting, courses, student interaction;
- Management training;
- Leading to graduate enterprise on the one hand and graduate recruitment on the other.

But underneath all this, it seemed that there is a lot of activity and energy expended, but without a clear vision for what one is trying to achieve.

There are both complimentary and conflicting goals, such as encouraging graduates into entrepreneurship courses, but actually seeing this as a means for enhancing employability. So, why do we need entrepreneurship skills? Do employers not want other skills more closely related to their own needs?

From being a collateral benefit, it has, in some institutions, become the reason for such activity and thus risks emptying the conceptual base of understanding the real-life world experiences of employees and entrepreneurs and in a way "mis-equipping" them.

There is little clarity about what the outputs are designed "to be" (e.g., graduate ventures; general education; business education; improved employability; enterprise skills. This lack of clarity about the intended outputs leads to significant diversity surrounding the inputs.

Although we can see that there are conceptual difficulties in the field, we recognise that this is a growth area, as stated earlier — society is moving on to embrace entrepreneurial behaviours, so it is now for the educationalists and trainers to develop programmes that meet the various needs.

Although for scholars the field can seem confusing, bearing in mind that society itself needs a great variety of individuals to fill its different needs, perhaps the fact that there is such a variety of offerings is a strength. The weakness may well be that the variety is an accident of incompetence and lack of understanding rather than a deliberate act of well-informed entrepreneurship educators.

In the next chapter, we have taken our own view of the way we think entrepreneurship education may be framed. In essence we see three major streams and a new entrant. The first might be described as formal education based around universities and being drawn from a long tradition of management education. This has resulted in many "how to books" as the content is distilled from more detailed curricula in universities. The second stream has been the growth of practitioner-led programmes that grew to cope with big social upheavals. These included many not-for-profit organisations. There is a third stream of skills-based training that has made its way into education. The fourth and most recent stream is the growth of TV format programmes that have captured the public's imagination in a great diversity of topics including singing, dancing, cooking, survival in the jungle to business ideas and employee effectiveness. These programmes may appear trivial to scholars in the field, but should not be underestimated for the impact they have on millions of viewers. The impact may be the creation of aspiration, signalling accepted behaviours, inspiration, desire for imitation, reduced fear of failure and other cultural influences that strengthens an extended society.

# Endnotes

1. Our thanks to Dr Joanna Mills who wrote much of this section as part of the teaching notes on an undergraduate course in entrepreneurship at the Centre for Entrepreneurial Learning.
2. W. Shalman, H.H. Stevenson, M.J. Roberts and A. Bhide (1999). *The Entrepreneurial Venture*, 2nd edition, Harvard Business School Press.
3. Adapted from Kirchoff, B.A. (1997). Entrepreneurship economics, In *The Portable MBA in Entrepreneurship*, W. Bygrave (ed.), Wiley, pp. 444–474.
4. G. Ibrahim, S. Vyakarnam. Defining the Role of the Entrepreneur in Economic Thought: Limitations of Mainstream Economics.
5. Schumpeter, J.A. (1934). *The Theory of Economic Development*. Harvard University Press.
6. Kirzner, I.M. (1973). *Competition and Entrepreneurship*. University of Chicago Press.
7. Knight, F.H. (1921). Risk, Uncertainty and Profit. Houghton Mifflin: Boston.
8. H. Stevenson (1983). A perspective on entrepreneurship. In *The Entrepreneurial Venture*, W. Sahlman *et al.* (eds.), 2nd edition., pp. 7–22, 1999. Harvard Business School Press.
9. J. Timmons (1999). *New Venture Creation: Entrepreneurship for the 21st Century*, 5th Edition, McGraw Hill, p. 46.
10. W. Bygrave (1997). *The Portable MBA in Entrepreneurship*, 2nd edition., Wiley.
11. S. Shane and S. Venkataraman (2000). The promise of entrepreneurship as a field of research. *Academy of Management Review* 25(1), pp. 217–226.
12. F. Moore (1986). Understanding entrepreneurial behaviour: A definition and model. *Academy of Management Proceedings*, pp. 66–70.
13. S. Shane and S. Venkataraman (2000) The Promise of entrepreneurship as a field of research. *Academy of Management Review* 25(1), pp. 217–226.
14. Karl H. Vesper and W. McMullan (eds.) (1988). Entrepreneurship: Today courses, tomorrow degrees? *Entrepreneurship Theory and Practice, 13*.
15. L. Pittaway and J. Cope (2007). Entrepreneurship education: A systematic review of the evidence. *International Small Business Journal* 25, pp. 479–510.

# Chapter 3

# Entrepreneurship Education is Not Just Strategy Made Simple!

This chapter briefly traces the origins of three sources of entrepreneurship education. We wanted to recognise these approaches as they influence the pedagogical developments in entrepreneurship education and development.

- The role of management and business education in creating content for managers and leaders
- Training for self-employment to cope with large-scale unemployment and underemployment in many countries
- Personal development for creating a more democratic society through leadership development, practical skills and community building

Each of these three origins to entrepreneurship education as we understand it today has lead to the creation and development of teaching materials, methods and frameworks for the future. We hope to lay the foundations in this chapter for the deeper description of our own work.

We develop a brief overview of these three sources of entrepreneurship education, taking a largely historical perspective, only to lay down the foundations for what we believe is the state-of-the-art. In Fig. 3.1, we add what we believe is a "left-field" new entrant to the whole spectre of entrepreneurship education — media television and (internet). We do not as yet know what the outcomes will be but describe them in this chapter.

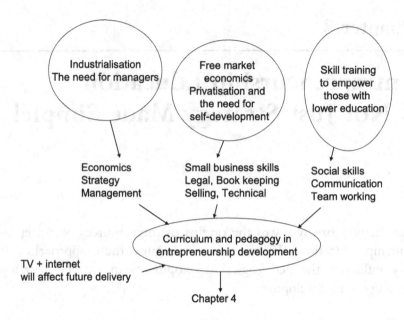

**Figure 3.1**   Summary of routes to the development of entrepreneurship education

## 3.1  Efficiency and Effectiveness

The early years of management, education and development focused on the supply of more effective and efficient managers — as loyal workers for large corporations. Many business schools and management departments were established alongside well-respected universities — Wharton, Harvard, Sloane, to name a few. The view held at the start of the 20th century was that large corporations brought about efficiencies of scale and that they were required to solve the big problems of the time; unemployment, and the need for infrastructure.

There were other "drivers" for such thinking — not least, Henry Ford's vision of producing cars on well-honed production lines. Industrialisation had started a century earlier in breaking up tasks into smaller units so that each member of the workforce could focus on a component part and become efficient.

Business schools were therefore influenced, in part, by the prevalent thinking in economics and responded to the needs of management, to find ways of understanding motivation (Maslow's hierarchy of needs), how and why workers respond to stimuli (Hawthorne studies), how to reward them (McClelland's need for achievement motivation), and how to manage them (McGregor's Theory X and Theory Y).

In addition to learning about how to manage people, students are also taught economics, strategy, marketing, finance, organisation theory, and more recently, technology (especially information technology).

Business schools are regarded as sources of senior managers capable of managing large enterprises. The curriculum, teaching methods (use of case studies), careers advice, and increasingly the international rankings are based on employability of its graduates. Increases in salaries on departure from their programmes and the level of prestige of the employer are two such indicators.

With the arrival of global quality standards for MBAs, there is increasingly little to differentiate institutions and their offering other than through the employability, quality of academic staff and softer indicators such as the ambience of the programme, its location and facilities.

In other words, it is becoming harder and harder to distinguish the content of management education from one institution to another. The dominant need is to equip its graduates for employment by larger (prestigious) organisations.

Derek Bok who was president at Harvard Business School questioned the purpose and direction of business education[1] in his book entitled *"Beyond the Ivory Tower: Social Responsibilities of the Modern University"* (1982). His question focused on understanding the ethical and corporate social responsibility of graduates. Therefore, the questions were not so much about how and why corporates benefited from recruiting the graduates as it was about how society benefits from such education. He has written many articles and books questioning the purpose of some of our more venerated institutions (not least government!). Some of the thought-provoking questions in his book of 1982 are still somewhat relevant today.

Bearing in mind the origins of management education — to find more efficient means of production and to gain competitive advantage in a free (global) market, the questions asked in the early half of the 20th century were not so much about entrepreneurship or innovation and even the great works of people like Schumpeter did not influence management education curriculum.

Instead, the thinkers at the time — including John K Galbraith — believed that the day of the small entrepreneur was over and that the future of free markets lay in the hands of large organisations. By implication, we needed to learn more about how to lead and manage such organisations and that these institutions were going to serve the needs of society.

We cannot be too critical of this line of thinking (in hindsight) because the world was emerging from food shortages, two world wars, huge reparation costs in Europe, debt burdens, and a cold war of ideologies, an arms race and a growing number of countries gradually gaining their independence from imperialism. Many countries were also starting to experience democratic systems while adopting planned supply side economics to overcome shortages and poor infrastructure.

These views take a fundamentally institutional view of the world. Therefore, people are seen as a resource to lead, manage and to be lead and managed for the greater good of the corporation. In a famous speech in 1953 when Charles Wilson moved from being president of General Motors to becoming Secretary of Defence, he responded to a question about conflicts of interest by saying: "What's good for General Motors is good for America".

Therefore, the view of management education as a mechanism of producing efficient and effective managers held for a long time, and even today is a dominant line of thinking in business schools and universities. This line of thinking influences curriculum, methods of teaching and the nature of research and publications.

## 3.2 Small is Beautiful

A different and more atomised view emerged in the mid-1970s from two unlikely sources. The first by the work of Schumacher in his seminal work entitled "*Small is Beautiful*".[2] This work was based on recognising the very large levels of unemployment and poverty across the world and that the focus on large-scale projects and organisations were creating a huge divide between those who had and those who did not have access to resources, wealth and basic needs.

His view was that individuals matter and by providing training, education and support to individuals you return their dignity to them and they can then work towards self-employment and become active members of the national economy.

> In 1955, Schumacher traveled to Burma as an economic consultant. While being there, he developed the principles of what he called "Buddhist economics", based on the belief that good work was essential for proper human development and that "production from local resources for local needs is the most rational way of economic life". (www.schumacher.org.uk)

These views were more in line with earlier philosophers like those of John Ruskin and Mahatma Gandhi than with Schumacher's early mentor — John Maynard Keynes. Sadly, Schumacher died in 1977, but by this time because he had been in influential positions in government and was a well-respected author and policy maker, his ideas started to take off and the result has been a huge growth in programmes to train people in self-employment.

The other unexpected ally was Mrs Thatcher, who came to power in 1979 and quite early on in her "reign", it became clear that she preferred private enterprise and celebrated individual responsibility. Her set of values took root alongside what became Reaganomics and together they forged ahead with promoting privatisation and free market economics. They were helped by the fuel and resultant economic crises of the time, whereby the International Monetary Fund (IMF) and World Bank no longer had an appetite to continue funding large-scale state-owned loss making businesses.

So, from the late 1970s and early 1980s, we began to see a surge of interest in privatisation and the impact around the world of self-employment programmes.[3] A sprinkling of these is highlighted in Table 1 below:

**Table 1**    Sample of Entrepreneurial Programmes since 1980s

| Country | Nature of programmes |
|---|---|
| United Kingdom (UK) | Overseas Development Administration — now the Department for International Development. Many programmes around the world on starting small companies, incubator infrastructure, training of trainers, creation and development of teaching materials. Conference sponsorships. |
| United States of America (USA) | USAID programmes. Similar to UK. |
| Germany | GTZ — promotion of intermediate technology, the development of technical training and transfer of technology. |
| Netherlands | Microcredit, village level and rural enterprise. |
| Sweden | Funding of programmes, academics supporting projects. |
| Canada | Funding programmes, academics supporting projects. |
| United Nations FAO; | All its various institutions were involved — ILO; UNDP; UNIDO — in programmes on gender equality, credit provision, infrastructure, etc. |
| World Bank | Through the IFC and with the IMF — major institutions continued to be funded and the provision of lines of credit for "SME development" through national banks. |
| Common Wealth Institute and related organisations | Exchanges between countries — South — South exchanges, training, market access, export encouragement, import substitution, technology transfer, etc. |

### 3.2.1  *What did all this Mean to Entrepreneurship Education?*

The largest impetus given to "SME" development, by the formal aid agencies was to take the educational materials from universities and business schools and convert these for the benefit of participants.

Bearing in mind that the materials in business schools had their origins in effective and efficient management rather than in venture creation; scholars, consultants and policy makers had to redevelop some of their thinking into what could work for start-ups.

In the end though, the vast majority of effort was about education that supported "business development" and we see in agency statements, bank literature and elsewhere the agonised definitions of SMEs — when in fact the target of their attention were people. This intellectual and psychological disconnect is probably an explanation as to why the billions of dollars in "SME development" has little to show for a more entrepreneurial culture in most countries as evidenced by the largest (and longest running) global study on entrepreneurship.[4]

## 3.3 The Menu

But what we do see is that the long endurance of management development, SME programmes and more recent courses in entrepreneurship has lead to a collection of approaches, a menu if you will, from which educators make choices for their various programmes and courses.

### 3.3.1 *Entrepreneurial Processes*

The dominant approach is entrepreneurial processes as summed up by Moore whose starting point was "past the idea generation". His focus being on "making it happen". Timmons' work is very similar but his work refers to "enactment". We described these in Chapter 2 and we suggest that they draw on the wisdom of business schools — where we might suggest that the content looks a bit like "strategy made simple" — as much of what is taught in entrepreneurship classes is also what is taught in MBA programmes in the mainstream of curriculum, but with an "entrepreneurial fizz".[5] Close examination of entrepreneurship materials from Stanford, Harvard and elsewhere illustrate a keen interest in implementation. They take for granted that the individuals with aspiration will come up with their own ideas. We now look at the vast menu of pedagogical approaches that have been used to transition from management education to enterprise education. This has been a valuable evolution and readers are encouraged to try as many as they can in their courses.

### 3.3.2 *Simulations*

There are many forms of simulation that can be used. They can be a powerful method, when the educational environment is short on time and needs methods that can form the basis of a useful set of lessons. Here are four examples:

1. *Creativity sessions that result in ideas to be taken forward.*
   This is quite labour intensive and requires group work as well as directed learning. The right environment has to be created in which individuals can be creative as well as learn about their creative ability. The ideal situation is that individuals and groups generate meaningful ideas.
2. *Writing business plans for ideas given to students.* An often used model in academic institutions is to teach people how to develop plans and bring the various strands together. The skills it develops include rigorous analysis, writing and communication, team work and "joined-up" thinking.
3. *Computer-based business simulations are available off the shelf and are used in time-constrained environments.* To be honest, these look outdated now compared to computer games in the games industry. Even Sim City for children has the same level of educational content as a sophisticated simulation from a university, but is more fun!
4. *Running a real business for a defined period of time.* Perhaps the most difficult to implement in most timetables, but they can be rich in lessons for individuals because of the real-life simulation they contain.

### 3.3.3 *Case Studies*

Case studies are frequently used in universities and in business schools. They are not easy to teach as the faculty member needs to have a deep insight in business and even the case itself. However, this model of teaching is prevalent and accompanied by teaching notes, is used very widely.

They are best used for efficient learning of certain key points, perhaps investment criteria, directors' duties, term sheets from venture capitalists, strategy, marketing plans, succession plans in growing companies and so forth. Case studies can rarely bring about the inner passion that individuals might have for their own ideas. Well-taught cases are long remembered and useful. They are highly "guru dependent".

Cases specially developed to highlight a particular lesson are perhaps the most powerful use of cases while the most passion and interest in a case and its lessons are those brought to class by students, that is, their own ideas and business plans.

### 3.3.4 *Metaphors*

It is sometimes hard to communicate new ideas, whether these are for business or for a new concept in terms of education. Hence, the use of metaphors can be truly helpful. Tutors need the skills to draw on metaphors and need to help students learn the benefits of such tools to describe their own ideas to audiences who might be skeptical. In other words, this is a form of communication skill that potential entrepreneurs need, to give themselves credibility with potential customers, investors and team members. An example might include "our business might look like Amazon, but for..." or "we will become the Southwest Airlines for Europe".

### 3.3.5 *Action Learning*

The essence of action learning[6] is to set questions or tasks for a team to solve. These need to be somewhat open-ended so that the team can work on the meaning of the question and set themselves a set of sub-routines that enable them to solve the question. Although first developed in large organisations for management development, this technique has wide application in entrepreneurship development as it is practical and highly interactive. A few examples are cited here:

- Creativity sessions — to solve a particular problem
- Project or business planning
- Building something — as part of a simulation
- Taking on a real project for a "client"
- Investigating the cause of a problem
- Conducting market research for a new product or service.

The key to setting up an action-learning environment is to be tolerant of ambiguity when setting the task, so as to allow students to discover and internalise more of the lessons for themselves. This can often be a challenge to individual tutors and to the institutions with targets to meet.

### 3.3.6 *Tasks as a Subset of Action Learning*

Simple classroom or group tasks are seen as a subset of action learning, where the latter builds on bigger (perhaps ambiguous) questions from which the groups can learn. Tasks, on the other hand, are very clearly defined routines.

These are important sources of exposure and experience for people to learn by doing and to build confidence to enable them to think and feel that they can achieve whatever they set out to do. So, for some people, overcoming shyness or inhibitions can be tackled through tasks.

It is also a good way to establish the desire and motivation to make things happen. Entrepreneurship is as much about doing as it is about the idea — so, enabling people to perform tasks within a safe environment is a great way to build confidence.

Typical tasks might include:

- Making short presentations, such as self-introduction;
- Team-building task that involves dexterity, thinking, planning and accessing resources;
- Understanding team roles, appreciating different roles as a debrief;
- Collaborating to complete a bigger task;

- Designing and performing a cabaret that brings together lessons from a course.

### 3.3.7 *Rich Pictures*

Providing delegates with colour pens, papers, etc., and giving them freedom to express themselves about conceptual ideas such as: personal motivations, values, ethics. These are really helpful in getting group discussions going as they dig underneath self-introductions and can take an ice-breaking session to a deeper level.

In entrepreneurship education, it may help to open up stereotypes, help to define entrepreneurship and what it means to people. This technique can also be used to unlock personal stories/backgrounds to help with building trust within a smaller environment and to encourage sharing.

Rich pictures are often used in training in post-conflict areas to help children recover from the traumas of violence, when they may not have the words to describe the horrors they have seen and experienced. It is a powerful tool and can be used quite simply in many environments.

### 3.3.8 *Reflections*

Individuals who are being encouraged to modify the way they think and their behaviours need to have time to reflect on what they have learnt and how they will internalise lessons/ideas. Time and tools for reflection, therefore, include:

- Quiet time with a diary or learning log. This requires absolute discipline.
- Writing a letter or note to oneself.
- Talking through the insights with a facilitator or mentor.
- Committing to a pledge to take action that comes from the desired new behaviours.

It is important in any learning environment to build in time for reflection, especially, with expectations of new behaviours.

### 3.3.9 *Standard Lectures*

Perhaps this is the most conventional way to deliver new information and insights, but nonetheless a very efficient method — and can be as interactive and lively as the speaker makes it.

This method is used by the tutor to cover information and concepts that are more easily taught through a standard lecture using boards, flip charts, presentations and the like. A very academic approach that may require prereading and group discussions.

When used by guest speakers, practitioners, they can also provide great role-model effects. There is a danger with guest speakers that they get onto a hobbyhorse of their own and do not respect the needs of the curriculum. Guest speakers need very careful management, both in terms of respecting their input and in ensuring that they deliver what is asked of them. The tutor typically places himself or herself in a "middle-man" position and care has to be taken.

Having raised the cautionary note, we are very much in favour of working with guest speakers to deliver practical tangible lessons because they bring with them a very high level of credibility, passion and can inspire students.

## 3.4 Personal Development Blended with Business Development

In the area of entrepreneurial learning, much of the content has been developed as a result of received wisdom from business schools and management development. There is a growing body of literature that entrepreneurial learning[7] needs to focus as much on personal development as on business development.

This would argue for a blended learning experience where business knowledge and skills are combined with the best of tools and approaches taken from training events.

But, we need to be able to draw on sound platforms of knowledge and understanding about personal development, otherwise risk a fair accusation that we are running events which result in a feel good factor but have no tangible outcomes that can be measured or related to any particular understanding of human aspirations, behaviours and motivation. In our work, we wish to draw on McClelland's achievement motivation and Bandura's self-efficacy theories.

## 3.5 Neighbouring Domains of Knowledge

While we build on these platforms, we also need to recognise other domains of knowledge that sit alongside our own and influence our work. These are the works of Polyani[8] — on tacit knowledge and Nahapiet and Ghoshal on social capital.[9]

Both of these are hugely influential in the practice of enterprise, because Polyani's work leads us to recognise that in entrepreneurship the educator cannot have answers to questions and that much of the information about opportunities, threats, resources and so forth lie outside the class room with networks of people and that to access these an individual needs to build on his or her social capital. We can transfer explicit knowledge somewhat more easily in formal education but tacit knowledge passes through a form of osmosis.

These are important theoretical frames of reference in designing entrepreneurship education because if we are to stimulate intent we also need to provide an ecosystem in which people can go forward by meeting potential team members, investors, suppliers, customers and others, through all of whom opportunities can be found and built on.

We describe it as building an ecosystem of opportunity and it requires careful design and orchestration, because as educators we have to go beyond the creation of content and delivery and also find ways of ensuring we are taking an ethical stance. After all, we are stimulating higher levels of aspiration and not everyone will be able to achieve their dreams!

## 3.6 So What?

Drawing together the three mainstream sources of education; industrialisation, SME development and training for skills, we can see why, people can get easily confused when trying to make sense of entrepreneurship education.

- Industrialisation brought us business and management studies in terms of curriculum, tool kits and trained people for analytical and strategy-making skills for big business. Largely led by universities and business schools.
- SME development has brought us a generation of role models, simple tools and training materials for start-ups and the management of smaller firms. It may also have left us with a legacy that entrepreneurship is about small business and therefore we also have to deal with this unworthy distinction. But let us come back to this later. SME development has been led and funded mainly by government agencies, not-for-profit organisations, banks and state agencies. In turn, they use universities and business schools as providers.
- Skills training, for example, in sales, communication, team formation, taking initiative, creativity, planning, project administration and so forth has given us a broad spectrum of approaches to use at grass-root levels. Mostly led by not-for-profit organisations and delivered mainly by trainers and consultants. Funded by regeneration budgets in inner cities, rural development, microfinance institutions and the like.

Each of these three sources has contributed to building entrepreneurship education, but none of them is complete and we need to find a model that brings together aspirations, with intent, skills, knowledge and current thinking on entrepreneurship development.

Meanwhile, for all that educators do, the gap is so wide in terms of provision that there is considerable degree of self-help in society. Some of the better-known models are described briefly.

## 3.7 Entrepreneurial Self-Help

As with all innovations and programmes, the real driving force for grass-root empowerment came from an outsider,[10] Dr Mohammed Yunus, who founded the Grameen Bank to provide microcredit to the poorest people so that they could lift themselves out of poverty. An entrepreneurial academic who has made a big difference to millions of people.

Over the years, we have seen (for example) projects such as:

- Young achievers from USA to celebrate the work of young people who have made a difference.
- Duke of Edinburgh Awards in the UK assists young people to take on personal challenges, whether these are physical or social and thus provides self-esteem opportunities.
- Young Enterprise — to inspire young people to gain an understanding of business, learn financial, social and leadership skills.
- Leadershape[11] has grown as a campus-based activity around universities to develop leadership qualities among graduates (more about this in the next chapter).
- There are many others focused on gender, unemployment, youth, homeless, rural, socially marginalised, refugee and a variety of other categories — all of which try and develop very basic commercial skills, together with the provision of technical skills and/or access to loans. See, for example, the work of GTZ — a German aid agency.[12]

These projects and those like it are in operation all over the world and are great sources of voluntary effort and bring about local impact. They are very practise based and do not pretend to have any academic foundation or theory from which they are derived.

However, there are a few Institutions around the world, such as the Entrepreneurship Development Institution (EDI) of India, that have embraced personal development at the heart of what they do. They have blended practise with theory. Much of what they have developed is derived from early work on motivation theories — such as those of McLelland (achievement motivation); E F Schumacher — ("small is beautiful") and their faculty are familiar with business development, banking principles and economics. Because their funding comes from the more formal institutions, they are also obliged to deliver "business ready" delegates.

### 3.7.1 *Television*

More recently, we have seen a secondary surge of public events, this time driven not by policy or educational institutions but by the media, ever hungry for new formats. So, we see television (TV) programmes like:

---

- Who Wants to Be     This has become a worldwide format and
  a Millionaire?        challenges people on general knowledge, with a big prize of cash and celebrity status as the attractions. People have to know their subjects to win and be able to cope with the stresses of TV.

- The Apprentice       Teams and individuals pitted against each other in a series of business tasks to gain an apprenticeship with a famous entrepreneur. The use of progressive elimination draws from earlier TV programmes.

- X-Factor            Talent shows, also based on public voting,
- Fame Academy      (using phone lines) to find people
- American Idol       with singing and dancing talent.
- So You Think You
  Can Dance
- Strictly Come
  Dancing
- Last Man Standing    This programme dares young men from the west to challenge their peers from the world's most remote tribes.

- Hells Kitchen       TV programme to train a number of hopefuls in preparing a meal for invited guests.

---

(*Continued*)

(*Continued*)

| | |
|---|---|
| • Many other kitchen/food programmes | There are a number of celebrity chefs, each with their idiosyncrasies, bringing about interest in health foods, quick cooking, specials diets and so forth. Some are entertaining and others mix this with a level of aspiration and education. |
| • Grand Designs | Follows people with grand ideas for individualising their homes. Looks at the highs and lows. Is largely celebratory. |
| • Dragons Den | This programme now attracts over 3 million viewers (in the UK) and is about entrepreneurs pitching their ideas to a group of investors. A quite remarkable format where pitching business ideas should become prime time TV. |
| • Big Brother | Perhaps the most brutal reality TV format around in seeking conflict and raising passions. Accompanied by pop-psychology analysis. In many ways quite dangerous but viewed by millions and discussed at length by future generations. Has this programme and others like it lead to an increased interest in psychology studies? |
| • How to Look Good Naked | These programmes are based on helping women look good and feel confident. |
| • Trinny and Susannah | They provide tips and guidelines on what works in terms of dress sense. |

These programmes tap into a competitive element, promote a high level of aspiration, the willingness to "have a go", endeavour and in many cases, down-to-earth practical lessons alongside (sometimes) wisdom. Their impact should not be underestimated. The so-called "elite" might sniff at the very idea that these programmes have anything to offer, but once we set aside any misgivings we have about the "brutality" of the way people are treated and they are sometimes treated in a callous manner — we can see there are significant lessons for personal development and education. It is outside the scope of this chapter to run into a review of TV programmes, but we encourage you to watch them in a dispassionate way and to go behind the entertainment to see and hear what goes on. We urge you to focus on the programmes linked to endeavour, business and decisions. Set aside the brutality of the entertainment and look instead at the questions and lessons on personal motivation, skills, application of expertise and knowledge.

What is truly fascinating about the surge in this format of programmes is how large the viewing numbers are and therefore how they tap into a pent up demand that we have not been able to satisfy through formal education.

We do not yet know whether this form of "edu-tainment" will overtake some of the so-called technical universities because of their ability to entertain and engage with their viewers. The faculty of these institutions now have to compete for the hearts and minds of their students against professional production presenters and celebrities.

Will they also make redundant some departments, books and scholars in certain disciplines? Will the formal education sector not have to respond to this left-field entrant?

## Endnotes

1. S. Vyakarnam (1986). The social relevance of management education: A case study of India. PhD thesis, Cranfield School of Management. http://ksgfaculty.harvard.edu/Derek_Bok
2. http://www.schumacher.org.uk/about_efschumacher.htm

3. S. Vyakarnam worked in this field from 1984 to 1999 — initially running two major programmes for advisors and educators of small businesses at Cranfield (DIGE) and later in Kenya (SEPP) with further projects for the World Bank, FAO, DfID and other agencies in India, South Africa, Tanzania, Kenya, Ghana. He has two earlier books based on his work and an internal publication for the FAO.

4. http://www.gemconsortium.org/

5. S. Vyakarnam recently attended as a guest — a Harvard case study discussion on an entrepreneurship module. The case was about strategy for a fast growth company and all the analytical tools used looked much like any other MBA class discussion.

6. The extensive work by Reg Revans provides useful backdrop to this approach.

7. D. Rae and M. Carswell (2001). Towards a conceptual understanding of entrepreneurial learning. *Journal of Small Business and Enterprise Development.*

8. L. Prusak (1997). Knowledge in Organizations. Chapter 7 by Polyani describes tacit knowledge in more detail.

9. Y.M. Myint, S. Vyakarnam and M. New (2005). The effect of social capital in new venture creation. The Cambridge High tech cluster. *Journal of Strategic Change.* This paper is based on the work of Nahapiet and Ghoshal to describe how social capital, both structural and social, has lead to a major entrepreneurial cluster. (J. Nahapiet and S. Ghoshal 1998). Social and intellectual capital and organisation advantage. *Academy of Management Review*, 23(2), 242–266.

10. http://www.grameen-info.org/

11. http://www.leadershape.org/home.asp

12. http://www.gtz.de/en/themen/wirtschaft-beschaeftigung/869.htm

# Chapter 4

# Bringing it All Together

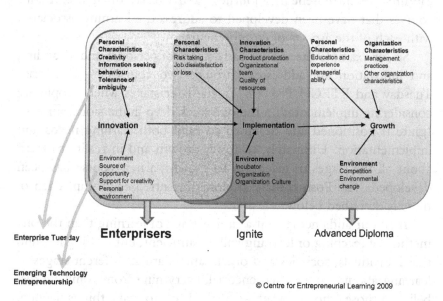

**Figure 4.1.** CfEL Programmes that help accelerate commercialisation of innovation.

First of all we need to admit that the concept of entrepreneurial learning remains largely undefined.[1] It has been variously described but for us its focus is on unlocking the combination of qualities that comes together to make new things happen. Our secondary aim is to try and inspire participants in believing in themselves so that they have the choice to make those "things" happen — whether these are new ventures, social projects or working more effectively for others in what they do — whether this is for society or an organisation.

If we are to embrace entrepreneurial learning, we need to embrace the notion that we are providing education "for" rather than "about" entrepreneurship and in this context the Centre for entrepreneurial Learning at University of Cambridge has developed a portfolio of courses that provide choices to those who are at different points on the learning curve of entrepreneurship. In Fig. 4.1, we capture the entrepreneurial journey[2] and overlay on it the various courses that have been developed to address the learning associated with each of the aspects of entrepreneurship.

So for example the various early stages of personal understanding and innovation are addressed through two courses — Enterprise Tuesday and ETECH Projects. In the later stages when people are considering implementation the one week deep immersion course — Ignite is positioned and designed to fulfil both learning needs and implementation. Ultimately, to foster growth and in reality to learn about all the stages of inception to growth, a new course has been developed: The Postgraduate Diploma in entrepreneurship. Each of these is described below.

If all our audiences are at a similar stage of learning then the one method of teaching or learning will be sufficient, but bearing in mind that individuals, societies and organisations are at different stages of learning about being entrepreneurial; everything from complete disbelief to those who are straining at the leash to make things happen, educators need to think about a portfolio approach to satisfy these different needs.

The main focus of this book is on Enterprisers, designed mainly to develop a high level of entrepreneurial intent, through building self confidence and making links through know how and skill development. It is a 4 day programme and acts as a springboard for change, as illustrated by some of the case studies in Chapter 8. But before we delve into the detail of how and when to run a programme like Enterprisers, this chapter provides a backdrop by outlining the portfolio at Cambridge.

One of the reasons for Enterprisers being what it is can be highlighted from a personal story of one of the authors:

On my annual trips to USA the one major thing that has become clear is that permission to "go for your dreams" is granted by society, so there is little need to have this as any part of an educational format. Instead, what is needed is to enable people to realise their dreams, hence there is focus on the development of social capital, business skills and know how. In the rest of the world there is much more evidence that we need to work with people in such a way that they can better understand themselves, learn about what motivates them, provide levels of self confidence and actually begin to realise that they do not need to seek permission. Better if they had the courage to seek forgiveness.

At the University of Cambridge it also became clear very early on in the life of the Centre for Entrepreneurial Learning that the graduates were being asked to do two new things that they had not fully bargained for when they signed up. Beyond their personal areas of domain expertise they were being asked to acquire "transferable skills" to become more relevant to future employers and to assist society at large through a rapid translation of research into products and services.

Both these challenges are forbidding to those who have actually signed up for a life in academia.

So we had to take a step back and lay on a course that created awareness and was based on inspirational role models, so that people could understand what it meant to have these skills and what it meant to commercialise knowledge. Our solution is "Enterprise Tuesday".

Another part of the learning is to ask when and how to determine whether research in the lab is ready for commercialisation. In addition we also need to build the skills, so people so that they can understand how to make that go/no-go decision. When is an idea a business opportunity? This is a thorny question and is much researched in entrepreneurship literature under the general heading of opportunity recognition and validation.

The learning opportunity is created by assigning small groups of students to projects that are in the "departure lounge" of the labs at

Cambridge. Students are expected to carry out a market feasibility study and report back to the "client researcher". But they actually do a lot more, because they have to start with understanding the science, whether competing solutions exist for the problem that is being addressed, the quality of publications, presence of patents in the core area and find time to think creatively to seek out the big opportunities. They are then expected to carry out some secondary and primary research; in the market place, identify competing solutions to the problems and which companies are in the sector. The also need to establish whether the 'client researchers' would have the appetite to take things forward.

The projects are presented back to the client researchers, thus providing scope for discussions and "education about entrepreneurship by stealth for the faculty". This course is now called ETECH Projects. It is run twice, once for undergraduates only with supervisions and mentoring by MBA students and once for MBA students who have doctoral students from science and engineering departments work with them in small teams.

For those who have a venture idea or project where they want to check out the feasibility while gaining the connections to help them take things forward, the CfEL devised, a one week deep immersion called Ignite. It attracts over 60 delegates a year from over a dozen countries to learn from and interact with around 120 of entrepreneurs, investors, lawyers, professional advisors, mentors and other business experts. This programme has lead to several companies being formed, money being raised, new business plans being developed and a range of other tangible connections have been made to further expand entrepreneurial ventures and alumni.

There is an enormous amount of goodwill in all entrepreneurial ecosystems and it is really up to those who orchestrate learning to come together with those who have experience to share what they know in structured and useful ways with future entrepreneurs. While this is possible and highly desirable in face to face sessions, we have found that there are frequently asked questions, common issues and the need for scalability that has encouraged us to increasingly video our speakers and invite specific interviews with selected entrepreneurs, so that we can disseminate more widely. This is an ongoing project and readers are invited to visit the CfEL website (resources) to access the videos.

## 4.1 Enterprise Tuesday

Enterprise Tuesday was designed for people who might ask the question: "What is entrepreneurship and is it for me?" In other words, it is an optional at open course aimed at graduates and postgraduates, to satisfy their curiosity.

There is an underpinning curriculum over a series of lectures, 12 in all that explores different facets of entrepreneurship such as personal motivation, circumstances, opportunity recognition and validation and more practical business and management issues such as strategy, marketing, team building, resource management and funding.

All the lectures are delivered by leading entrepreneurs, investors and professionals, often as panel sessions, to provide diversity of views and experiences. Every lecture session is followed by networking. These are sponsored and so enable people to stay back and mingle.

In addition to the students and staff of the University, Enterprise Tuesday is open to neighbouring Universities and to the business community. The audience mix and diversity includes around 30% to 40% non-University participation from the local business community, entrepreneurs and professional service providers.

This diversity of audience is quite central to the University playing an important role for the region and is a good example of demonstrating how the University can be seen to be a regional resource in enterprise and innovation.

Enterprise Tuesday plays a pivotal role for awareness-raising and promotion for two student societies to make connections and generate memberships. These are CUE (business creation competition) and CUTEC (technology venture conference). In fact many business teams have formed out of the networking sessions that follow each lecture, the most recent example being "i-Solve" — which combines two undergrads from Computer Science and one MBA. They won the software prize for 2009 in the CUE Business Creation competition.

### 4.1.1  *Evolution of Enterprise Tuesday*

Enterprise Tuesday has grown from an open course within the University, delivering the basics of building a business to around 30–40 students into an open programme that now has a total registered base of around 2000 people, attracting audience sizes of up to 350 on a busy night. Enterprise Tuesday has gained a durability and embeddedness that other lecture series in entrepreneurship have not managed. A key element to this durability is the consistency of the programme leadership, design and delivery.

Enterprise Tuesday has generated a very high level of good will of the people that come and speak. We draw in very inspirational people at no financial cost bar a small gift and coverage of expenses, and many come back year after year.

All lectures are now videoed and are available as open source via the CfEL website. This is becoming a wonderful resource through the high quality and standards of the speakers.

Enterprise Tuesday has also been a source of inspiration to other Universities that have since copied the format. This includes the Universities of Essex, Bedford, East Anglia, Hertfordshire, Sussex, Reading, Oxford, University of the Sunshine Coast, [Australia], Laurea University of Applied Sciences, [Finland] and from time to time we hear anecdotal evidence of yet more courses styled on Enterprise Tuesday (the latest being from Malaysia — University of Kelantan). CfEL is very happy with this element of outreach as it enables an increasing number of people to take part in entrepreneurship courses without using up any of the resources at CfEL. Information on how to run and further develop formats of Enterprise Tuesday is freely shared.

### 4.2  Operational Elements

The following resources are required to run a typical series each year:

1. A marketing budget that allows for a leaflet to be printed, web development, regular press releases and on-line promotion.

2. Poster and leaflet distribution across the University and the various business organisations around Cambridge.
3. Large scale mailings outside the City of Cambridge.
4. An audio/visual staff member, who records all the lectures, edits and uploads the final cut.
5. The programme manager who works with the Director to secure speakers from suggestions and networking activities. This cycle of activity runs between January and June each year.
6. Drive to secure additional sponsorship to cover some of the costs that arise over and above staff costs and overheads.
7. A rota arrangement within CfEL to staff each of the 12 evenings, including a mix of overtime and time-off in lieu payments.
8. Additional staff to provide for the physical movement of food and drink and all the kit that has to be taken from storage to the venue and back each week.
9. Presents and travel reimbursements for speakers.
10. Internal meetings with the teams from student societies to ensure smooth running of each event.
11. Registrations, data gathering, reporting on Enterprise Tuesday.

### 4.2.1 *Overall Cost Elements of Enterprise Tuesday*

1. One Full time equivalent for the Programme management and AV production.
2. Marketing staff costs, printing and production.
3. Food and drink (funded through sponsorships).
4. Photography — for use in PR.
5. Travel and presents for speakers.
6. Various consumables.
7. Overtime, casual labour and time off in lieu for 12 evenings.

Figure 4.2 shows how Enterprise Tuesday has grown over the last 9 years from modest beginnings to a current registration base of nearly 2000 registrants. Enterprise Tuesday is the most popular non-assessed course within the University.

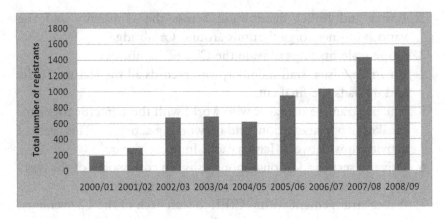

**Figure 4.2.**    Increase in Registrations over 9 years.

## 4.2.2  ETECH Projects

This course evolved from an undergraduate course on entrepreneurship in the Physics Department of the University of Cambridge. The transition to the present design and structure arose from the convergence of a number of elements:

The course grew to service three Departments; Physics, Materials Science and Chemical Engineering. Each Department was being served with lectures, course work, assessment and it became clear that the University needed to merge the teaching, perhaps retaining a level of customisation in favour of each department.

On the MBA programme at the Business School, the growth of interest in entrepreneurship meant that a new course on business planning was introduced and with a new vision/direction that the Business School would work at the heart of the University, it became obvious that new ways of engaging the MBA students with the wider University would be welcomed.

At the same time, Cambridge Enterprise (the technology transfer office of the University) was increasing awareness of the potential for technology transfer and commercialisation of intellectual property. The University of Cambridge has a strong research base and there is an increasing level of engagement in the commercialisation agenda. It also has a strong pool of students as a "free resource".

So by joining these dots — availability of leading edge research, project based learning for students and a common teaching platform, it has become possible to develop a course with practical real-life outputs that provide a number of benefits:

Students learn about opportunity recognition and how to conduct commercial feasibility studies on disruptive and emergent technologies. They also learn market research skills, presentations of commercial information and working on projects in small teams.

Faculty obtain practical reports to help them consider the reality of commercialising their research outputs.

Cambridge Enterprise sees slightly more considered requests for commercialising technology from the faculty. This ultimately can reduce time and resources allocated to early stage filtering of requests for IP protection.

The University benefits from an increased deal flow and the wider society gets people who are better trained at being able to recognise technology based opportunities and to ask the right questions about the feasibility of going to market.

The course evolution is depicted in Figure 4.1 below. Its growth in terms of student numbers is still in its infancy relative to what can be achieved (Figure 4.2) due to complexities in scheduling, assessment and inclusion into curricula that are highly established and mature. In Figure 4.3, we summarize the technologies that have so far been assessed.

### 4.2.3 *Ignite*

Ignite is an intensive, one week programme for aspiring entrepreneurs and corporate innovators to trial and prepare business ideas for commercialisation. It is comprised of a blend of practical teaching, expert clinics, mentoring sessions and experienced advice and support from leading entrepreneurs, investors, business angels, professional service providers.[4] Further detailed and up to date information is available via www.cfel.jbs.cam.ac.uk.

Ignite is a rather special programme in the entrepreneurial calendar because it brings together a diverse mix of people, activities and

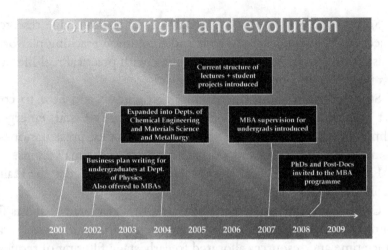

## 400+ students taught to date

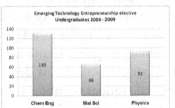

- More than **105 MBAs** in total
- Around **10** PhDs in 2008 and 2009
- Approx **35** student projects on commercial due diligence

- More than **285** undergraduates in total
- Approx **65** student projects on commercial due diligence

## 50+ novel technologies assessed

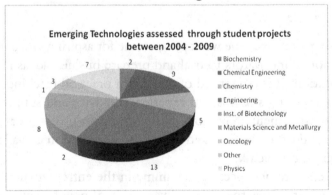

tasks to enable delegates to robustly develop their thinking for ideas they bring with them to the programme. It is aimed at technology (and biotech) business creation projects from large corporations, Universities and public research Institutions, small venture capital backed firms and the one man band. It is not the who you are that matters to this programme, more the "what you want to do" that defines selection and participation.

So the programme includes:

- Access to the Cambridge Entrepreneur Network
- One week, intensive, "hothouse" environment
- Acceleration of the validation and commercialisation process
- Tailored support specific to project needs
- International links
- On-going support and advice

The programme aims to help delegates achieve:

- Inspiration, motivation and the tools required to take the next steps in terms of commercialising ideas and progressing internal ventures and projects
- Key skills, motivation and contacts to allow the organisation to exploit new ideas in response to customer needs more effectively
- The identification of good opportunities in a short period with minimal investment
- Improve communication and understanding between the technical and sales team
- Increase enthusiasm for innovation within the team

The key outcomes for the programme include

- Learning how to explain the technology opportunity in commercial terms
- A commercial approach in the development of innovative ideas
- Clarification of the business idea, having tested it within a high calibre and safe environment

- A significant network of contacts with the business community, Cambridge investor network and peers from Ignite
- Thinking time

Track record so far for Ignite includes

- Over 400 participants from 25 countries across Europe, Asia and the Americas since the programme started in 1999. The alumni are made up of people from various disciplines and industry sectors, such as bioscience, physics, engineering and computer sciences. Over 55 businesses have been developed and more than £85 million in funding has been raised by alumni in the period from 1999–2009.

### 4.2.3.1 *Guiding principles for Ignite*

One of our core values is to involve experienced and new entrepreneurs, practitioners and service providers in the delivery of all programmes, as they have the credibility to teach entrepreneurship through sharing their own experiences and knowledge and inspiring future entrepreneurs. This creates direct links between students and the business community.

All the contributors to the Ignite week are actively involved in the creation and development of new ideas and ventures. In all, there are around 120 Contributors; most of them being leading entrepreneurs, innovators and professionals who have gone through similar types of experiences that delegates are currently facing.

In operational terms it is a major exercise. While the overall curriculum was set some time ago, to contain keynote talks on vision, strategy and marketing, funding, teams and deal making, there are workshops, small group mentoring sessions, clinics, surgeries, dinners, networking events and poster sessions that deal with the myriad elements of tacit knowledge. By having such an intensive week and hosting 120+ local practitioners the programme seeks to provide both high level generic information about how to convert an idea into a venture and the detailed personal mentoring that is possible by including people from business. Ignite also attracts a volunteer group of about 20 MBAs each year from the University of Cambridge, Judge Business School who provide very hands on assistance to get market research done, analyse the opportunity, develop presentations and provide other support as needed (not least a bit of social time too). In due course links are made, job opportunities created and important introductions are provided and the sense among participants is that they "get their money back" with in a few days of attendance!

As might be expected of such an event, planning starts months in advance and the main operational issue is to get the right people to the right place, ensure effective marketing and carry out the detailed event management that is needed for any big conference.

## 4.3 Postgradute Diploma in Entrepreneurship

This is a new programme, and for the purposes of this book it is sufficient at this stage to say that the four module programme is designed to strengthen the ability of people to not only begin an entrepreneurial journey but to also grow their own ventures and themselves. Three of the modules include residential sessions in Cambridge, and the remainder is delivered on-line through a virtual learning environment. The objectives are to lay down a foundation of understanding theory in the practise of entrepreneurship and then follow this with courses, tasks and tutoring to enable students to simultaneously progress their venture ideas and their learning about entrepreneurship.

The long term plans are to make this a significantly large programme.

### 4.3.1 *Enterprisers*

The next few chapters develop a more detailed description of Enterprisers. We simply acknowledge in this chapter that Enterprisers plays a key role in the portfolio of programmes at CfEL in providing content and process to enable the development of self confidence, self belief through a high intensity four day course that helps to unlock creativity, team working, idea generation and validation and learning how to present different ideas to strangers. It also combines networking and the development of social skills. Increasingly we find that students participate on Enterprise Tuesday and Enterprisers. Some of them return to take up E-TECH projects and Ignite and for those few who do the full journey they would have benefitted from the complete learning journey of entrepreneurial processes.

## Endnotes

1. P. Diamanto (2005). The process of entrepreneurial learning: a conceptual framework. Entrepreneurship Theory and Practise, pp. 40–49, July.
2. F. Moore (1986). Understanding entrepreneurial behaviour: A definition and model. *Academy of Management Proceedings,* pp. 66–70.
3. Figures courtesy of Arum Muthirulan, Programme Manager at CfEL.
4. The text for the description is taken from the www.cfel.jbs.cam.ac.uk website and adapted for this chapter.

# Chapter 5

# Enterprisers — A Bold Experiment

The first three chapters provide an examination of how we have thought about and taught entrepreneurship. In 2000, the British Government provided funding to create the Cambridge-MIT Initiative, directing members of the University of Cambridge and the Massachusetts Institute of Technology to consider how the spirit of entrepreneurship could be developed and nurtured throughout the United Kingdom. Numerous programmes, projects, and collaborations developed over the next several years and this chapter focuses on one of those programmes — CMI-Connections — now called Enterprisers.

## 5.1 A Brief History

Interested parties at Cambridge and MIT pondered the question about teaching entrepreneurship in an intensive programme. We looked at an existing programme at MIT — MIT LeaderShape — as a starting point.

MIT LeaderShape is a partnership between MIT and LeaderShape Inc., a non-profit organisation in Champagne, Illinois. LeaderShape Inc., provides the complete curriculum for MIT LeaderShape and other campus-based LeaderShape sessions nationwide.

The programme, which came to MIT in 1995, is designed to develop a number of skills in problem solving, professional ethics and decision making. It includes a variety of topics and activities, including action planning, team building, group decision making and conflict resolution. Sustained faculty–student interaction is central to the experience and most decisions and activities take place in small "clusters", which provide supportive, safe environments that promote learning and develop new skills and attitudes.

LeaderShape is an intensive 6-day leadership-development and community-building experience. Each participant creates an individual plan of action, the hallmark of the LeaderShape curriculum. Each plan of action is designed to bring positive change to the campus community and is implemented during the following academic year.

## 5.2  CMI-Connections is Born

Following the innovative structure of LeaderShape, we considered if such an approach could apply to entrepreneurship education and created the first iteration of CMI-Connections. Connections was chosen based on the idea that connections are an important thread for entrepreneurs and the programme would connect like-minded people with a variety of academics, entrepreneurs and others.

CMI-Connections was established as a bold experiment to see what would happen when you take talented people from all corners of the globe, each with diverse cultural backgrounds and disciplines, and combine this with an experience in entrepreneurship education over a week-long residential retreat. Academics have long debated whether or not you can teach entrepreneurship; we believe entrepreneurship can be taught, but question what we were trying to achieve in terms of learning outcomes.

Our conclusions so far are that entrepreneurship teaching comes down to two broad areas: business knowledge and personal development. They are interconnected, and expertise in one area with insufficient development in the other will result in an incomplete "Enterpriser". What we have discovered, and what is supported by the research, is that CMI-Connections (now Enterprisers) raises participants' levels of self-confidence and self-belief, which in turn can raise their entrepreneurial intent.

### 5.2.1  *The Programme Evolves — Connections to Enterprisers*

During the period from 2002 to present, CMI-Connections changed to its current name of Enterprisers, better reflecting the nature of the programme. Originally conceived as targeting university undergraduate students, Enterprisers has now been delivered to undergraduate students, PhD students, university faculty and to corporate audience. Programmes have been conducted throughout England, in Scotland, and in Australia.

The full range of programmes delivered includes:

| Host College/Institution | Location | Date |
|---|---|---|
| MIT & Cambridge | Boston, Massachusetts, USA | 2002 |
| Van Mildert College, University of Durham | England | 2003 |
| University of Strathclyde | Glasgow, Scotland | 2003 |
| Van Mildert College, University of Durham | England | 2004 |
| Heriot-Watt University | Edinburgh, Scotland | 2004 |
| Van Mildert College, University of Durham | England | 2005 |
| University of Sussex | Brighton, England | 2005 |
| Roehampton University | London, England | 2005 |
| Van Mildert College, University of Durham | England | 2006 |
| University of Sussex | Brighton, England | 2006 |
| Van Mildert College, University of Durham | England | 2007 |
| University of the Sunshine Coast | Australia | 2007 (Jan) |
| Microsoft | London, England | 2007 |
| University of the Sunshine Coast | Australia | 2007 (Sept) |
| Van Mildert College, University of Durham | England | 2008 |
| Evonik | Marl, Germany | 2008 |
| Microsoft | London, England | 2008 |
| Judge Business School | Cambridge, England | 2008 |
| Arden Training Centre | Warwick, England | 2009 |
| University of Cambridge | Cambridge, England | 2009 |
| University of Newcastle | Cambridge, England | 2009 |

The Enterprisers programme is about many different things:

- Getting to know one another
- Learning about yourself and how to be enterprising
- Exploring entrepreneurship in ways that aren't often covered in textbooks and classroom activities
- Developing an entrepreneurial project plan and learning what you need to know to maximise your success in implementing the plan

## 5.3  The Enterprisers Journey

The Enterprisers Journey each day builds upon each previous day as an integrated learning experience moving on from "Here I Am"; the output of day 1 when we are looking to the entrepreneur within, to "My Idea"; learning how to spot new opportunities and enhance existing ideas, to "My Plan"; when we address how to pitch participants' ideas and plan ahead for the future.

More detail on this process follows:

### 5.3.1  *Day One — Moi*

"The entrepreneur within" is all about understanding personal values and direction; unleashing the enterpriser within each of us and community building. Putting all this in the context of entrepreneurship, we present the idea that in life if one is going to do something one might as well make a difference, make one's mark by thinking big. Thinking beyond moi, the end of the first day involves a cultural simulation called BaFa BaFa.

### 5.3.2  *Day Two — Ideation*

"Launching a great idea" is about better understanding what an entrepreneur is and does. The aim of this day is to give participants practical tools, enjoyable experiences and confidence in spotting and developing ideas for entrepreneurship and enterprise. One learns about how to effectively work in different environments and in teams. Putting people and society at the heart of new ventures is critical and the end of day two is sometimes rounded off by considering business and personal ethics.

### 5.3.3 *Day Three — Nuts'n'Bolts*

"What will it take to succeed?" This question leads to critically important questions such as: Is there a market for your idea? How are you going to finance it? And how are you going to plan the steps needed to get going? To help individuals focus their plan, we invite a number of entrepreneurs to tell their stories, emphasising both failures and successes. These entrepreneurs are from a spectrum of stages — new starts to serial entrepreneurs — and walks of life — academic to social entrepreneurs and corporate innovators. Networking with entrepreneurs ends the day, offering opportunities to practice networking over dinner and throughout the evening.

### 5.3.4 *Day Four — Crystal Ball*

"Keeping the dream alive" is about motivation, sustaining commitment, planning how to best move forward as a community and celebrating the experience.

## 5.4 Enterprisers Timetable

Enterprisers is typically a 4-day intensive programme, but it has been tailored into a 3-day event for certain groups. It is crucial to recognise that the programme is designed as an intensive experience, starting activities in the early morning and running into the evening, and that the social aspect of the programme contributes significantly to the development of confidence and sense of community.

The programme is specifically designed to provide both large-group and small-group activities and the content allows for participants to move through the process of the 4 days. In many ways, everything builds on what has come before.

Chapter 6 provides details about each of the activities and exercises included in the Enterprisers programme, but we provide a general description of the 4 days here.

Day one, *Moi*, focuses on understanding personal values and direction. It is also critical for establishing the tone and atmosphere for the programme. The following activities and exercises occur during the first day:

- Welcome and introductions (large group);
- Personal goals (small groups);
- Getting to know you (small groups);
- Reflections (small or large group);
- Bafa bafa (or other cultural simulation) (large group).

Day two, *Ideation*, introduces participants to what an entrepreneur is, and does, and creates opportunities to learn how to work effectively in different environments and in teams. The programme involves the following experiences:

- Co-operate (small groups);
- Co-operate (small groups with debrief in large group);
- Inspiring ideas (large group introduction; work in small groups);
- Reflections (small or large group);
- Ethics (large group).

Day three, *Nuts 'n' Bolts*, asks critical questions about the marketability of ideas, financing options and how to get started. Activities during day three include:

- Creating a business plan (small groups, but in one setting);
- Raising finance (large group);
- Markets approach (large group);
- Networking skills (large group);
- Entrepreneurship panel (large group);
- Networking with entrepreneurs (during dinner and beyond).

The final day, *Crystal Ball,* really considers how to keep the motivation going. Activities include:

- Pitching ideas (small groups);
- Pitching to the panel (large group);
- Keeping the dream alive (large group);
- Cabaret preparation (small groups);
- Cabaret (large group) and
- Optional gala dinner (large group celebration).

## 5.4.1 *Social Aspects*

Interactions among programme participants and facilitators are an important part of the Enterprisers programme and these tend to occur in three primary settings: meals, breaks and in the pub or similar location.

Breakfast, lunch and dinner provide opportunities to meet a number of programme participants during the week. We generally schedule each meal for 1 hour to allow for conversation and exchange of ideas.

As long as 30-minute breaks are generally scheduled each morning and afternoon during the programme. These breaks help to revive energy levels as well as promote conversation.

There is an activity scheduled each evening following dinner that keeps everyone engaged until approximately 9:00 p.m. We actively seek venues for Enterprisers that have an on-campus or on-location pub or similar facility where everyone can meet informally following the day's activities. This has proven to be highly successful for creating a strong sense of community.

### 5.4.1.1 *Rules of engagement*

There are typically around 64 participants in a university-level Enterprisers programme, coupled with 14–16 facilitators, 2 lead facilitators, and a staff who keep everything organised and functioning. Anytime a large group comes together, it is helpful to have a simple set of ground rules and Enterprisers has developed five such rules to allow everyone to get the most out of the programme:

(1) **We are all here to learn.**
While at various times different people will be leading discussions or offering ideas to consider, this does not mean that learning only happens one way. We are all teachers and learners and we have much to learn from one another.

(2) **We are all here to participate in the week.**
Participation doesn't mean talking all the time — we can participate through active listening, carefully hearing what is being said and having an open mind. One's presence is expected — always. Whether in the large group or in a one-on-one setting, everyone must be committed to being present in order for this week to be meaningful.

(3) **We are all here to get something new, not the "right" answers.**
Assuming agreement that we are all here to learn, that means we are all here to get something new. Active listening involves having an open mind. Getting something new requires that as well — having an open mind allows new ideas to flow in. Although we may not agree with everything we hear this week, having an open mind at least allows one the chance to contemplate new ideas. Getting something new often requires giving something of yourself. Do not hold back — contribute ideas, ask questions, wonder thoughts aloud.

(4) **We will get the most out of the week by valuing and respecting diversity and each other.**
We have brought together students, faculty and staff from multiple universities and backgrounds because we learn more when we have the opportunity to look at ideas from different points of view. It is crucial that we support the diversity we have by respecting each other and the ideas and opinions we share. We don't always need to agree, but we always need to respect each other.

(5) **Each of us has the talent and skills to be a successful entrepreneur.**
Entrepreneurship, as we define it, is about unlocking and unleashing every person's potential to (1) create bold visions

for changes they want to see in the world and new opportunities they want to seize, (2) develop well-structured plans to turn these visions into reality and (3) work with and through others to leverage resources needed to achieve success.

### 5.4.1.2 *Student selection — Some considerations*

Let us focus here on selection criteria and processes for university-level Enterprisers programmes.

In our experience, 64 participants is an ideal number. This allows for a significant amount of diversity, including such factors as academic disciplines, countries of origin, and gender, racial, and ethnic mixes. As many as 64 participants also allows for the creation of 8 small groups with 8 members each, led by 2 facilitators.

This also allows anywhere from 8 to 12 universities to select and send students to the Enterprisers programme. It is useful to establish an application process, while leaving the interview and selection process up to each participating institution. Guidelines must be established so that everyone involved in the selection process understands what types of students would both contribute to and gain the most from Enterprisers.

### 5.4.1.3 *Choosing a venue*

Enterprisers works successfully as an intensive, residential programme and selecting an appropriate venue is critical. When possible, it is helpful to choose a site that is removed from local distractions. The venue needs to provide appropriate accommodations for students and facilitators. Dining facilities must allow for easy communication and provide meal choices suitable for the participants.

Meeting spaces are important for the various activities and exercises. There must be a large space for sessions with the whole group and the necessary number of break-out rooms for the small-group meetings. Aesthetic appeal should be considered — participants will be in these spaces for four days and nights.

## 5.5 The Overarching Goal of Enterprisers

It is useful to recognise that Enterprisers is trying, more than anything else, to raise the participants' levels of self-confidence and self-belief, which in turn can raise their entrepreneurial intent.

This is achieved through a mix of tools, interventions and activities that are incorporated into the programme. This outcome of raised levels of entrepreneurial intent is not only for starting businesses, but also to encourage people to innovate, get social enterprises underway and to have a greater capacity to go forward in their careers. We have based this set of outcomes on the work of Bandura:[1]

> "Important in the decision to start a venture is the confidence and self-belief that an individual or group of potential founders has in their ability to undertake successfully the many sub-actions/activities that are required. Self-efficacy is central to the willingness to act in an entrepreneurial way, to identify and seize opportunities. First postulated by Bandura[2] self-efficacy beliefs are 'people's judgment of their capabilities to organise and execute courses of action required to produce given attainments' and have the consequences that 'people's level of motivation, affective states, and actions are based more on what they believe than on what is objectively true'."[3]

### Endnotes

1. Albert Bandura, 1925-present.
2. A. Bandura (1997). *Self-Efficacy: The Exercise of Control.* New York: Freeman.
3. William Lucas and Sarah Cooper, Hunter. Enhancing self-efficacy to enable entrepreneurship: the case of CMI Connections. Paper presented to: High-Technology Small Firms Conference, the 12th Annual International Conference at the University of Twente Enschede, The Netherlands (Year).

| Enterpriser lessons and how it fits together | Main outcomes | Duration | Self-awareness | | | Business awareness | | | Confidence building | | Inspiration |
|---|---|---|---|---|---|---|---|---|---|---|---|
| | | Mins | Ice breaker | Knowledge | Skills | Ice breaker | Knowledge | Skills | Skills | Practise | |
| Lines lines Lines, include where people are from | break the ice, get to meet people, fun | 30 | ✓ | | | | | | | | |
| Human map | speaking — beat up in public, get an impression of cultural diversity | | | | | | | | | | |
| Personal goals — introduction | Get an understanding of the programme, code of conduct, expectations, set the tone | 30 | | ✓ | | | ✓ | | | ✓ | ✓ |

(Continued)

| Enterpriser lessons and how it fits together | Main outcomes | Duration | Self-awareness | | | Business awareness | | | Confidence building | | Inspiration |
|---|---|---|---|---|---|---|---|---|---|---|---|
| | | Mins | Ice breaker | Knowledge | Skills | Ice breaker | Knowledge | Skills | Skills | Practise | |
| Coat of arms | Start to look at themselves for the first time, explain themselves in small groups | 60 | | ✓ | | | | | | | |
| Time line | Log their achievements — sense of self-esteem | 30 | | ✓ | | | | | | | |
| Dance card networking | Continue to meet others | 60 | | | ✓ | | | | | | |
| Creativity | Acquire skills in creativity and ideation | 180 | | | ✓ | ✓ | ✓ | | | ✓ | |
| Time out to create ideas | Move from generic to specific | 180 | | | ✓ | | ✓ | | | ✓ | |

(Continued)

| Enterpriser lessons and how it fits together | Main outcomes | Duration | Self-awareness | | | Business awareness | | | Confidence building | | Inspiration |
|---|---|---|---|---|---|---|---|---|---|---|---|
| | | Mins | Ice breaker | Knowledge | Skills | Ice breaker | Knowledge | Skills | Skills | Practise | |
| Cultural awareness | Understand other cultures and what drives them — raising awareness | 90 | | ✓ | ✓ | | | | | | |
| Team roles | Team building | 180 | | | | | ✓ | | | | |
| Grand visionary | Peer learning that it is OK to think big | 120 | | | | | | | ✓ | ✓ | ✓ |
| Ethics | Put enterprise in context that it is expected to be ethical while trying to achieve self-awareness | 90 | | ✓ | | | | | | | |
| Business strategy | Project and business planning. Language of business | 120 | | | | | ✓ | ✓ | | | |

(Continued)

| Enterpriser lessons and how it fits together | Main outcomes | Duration (Mins) | Self-awareness Ice breaker | Self-awareness Knowledge | Self-awareness Skills | Business awareness Ice breaker | Business awareness Knowledge | Business awareness Skills | Confidence building Skills | Confidence building Practise | Inspiration |
|---|---|---|---|---|---|---|---|---|---|---|---|
| Markets | Analytical tool to assess new ideas | 60 | | | | | ✓ | | | | |
| Finance | Language of finance and key issues for new project/business formation | 90 | | | | | ✓ | | | | |
| Panel of entrepreneurs | Tacit knowledge about business | 120 | | | | | | ✓ | | ✓ | ✓ |
| Networking dinner — Gala | First formal setting — getting students used to the idea of business networking | 120 | | | | | | | ✓ | ✓ | ✓ |

(*Continued*)

| Enterpriser lessons and how it fits together | Main outcomes | Duration | Self-awareness | | | Business awareness | | | Confidence building | | |
|---|---|---|---|---|---|---|---|---|---|---|---|
| | | Mins | Ice breaker | Knowledge | Skills | Ice breaker | Knowledge | Skills | Skills | Practise | Inspiration |
| Pitching | Practise at succintly putting ideas forward — to get buy-in | 120 | | | ✓ | | | ✓ | | ✓ | |
| Wrap up — making promises | Taking all that they have learned and setting out a promise to do something with it | 90 | | ✓ | | | | | | | |
| Cabaret preparation | Final fun team work, fusing creativity, lessons for the week and presentation skills | 120 | | | ✓ | | | | ✓ | ✓ | |

(*Continued*)

| Enterpriser lessons and how it fits together | Main outcomes | Duration | Self-awareness | | | Business awareness | | | Confidence building | | Inspiration |
|---|---|---|---|---|---|---|---|---|---|---|---|
| | | Mins | Ice breaker | Knowledge | Skills | Ice breaker | Knowledge | Skills | Skills | Practise | |
| Cabaret | Final team delivery of a finished "product" and having fun | 120 | | | | | | | | ✓ | |
| Optional final dinner | Forming final networks and communities | 120 | | | | | | | | | ✓ |
| Reflections book | Learning to learn about self, taking down tips and pointers | 60 | | ✓ | | | | | | ✓ | |
| Informal learning time | Consolidating what has been in the formal sessions, building confidence and being able to think outside the box | | ✓ | ✓ | | ✓ | ✓ | | ✓ | | ✓ |
| Total units | | 2280 | 2 | 9 | 6 | 2 | 7 | 4 | 4 | 9 | 6 |

| | Day 1 Moi | Day 2 Ideation | Day 3 Nuts 'n' bolts | Day 4 Crystal ball |
|---|---|---|---|---|
| 08:00 | Breakfast | Breakfast | Breakfast | Breakfast |
| 08:45 | | Daily briefing | | Daily briefing |
| 09:00 | Facilitators training | Co-operate | Daily briefing | Pitching |
| 10:30 | | Pit stop | Business strategy | |
| 11:00 | Registration and check-in | Co-operate | Pit stop | Pit stop |
| 11:30 | Welcome and introductions | | Raising finance | Presenting to the panel |
| 12:00 | | | | |
| 12:30 | Lunch | Lunch | Lunch | Lunch |
| 13:30 | | Inspiring ideas | Markets approach | |

(Continued)

| | Day 1 Moi | Day 2 Peopleology | Day 3 Nuts 'n' bolts | Day 4 Crystal ball |
|---|---|---|---|---|
| 14:30 | Pit stop | | Networking skills | Keeping the dream alive |
| 15:00 | Personal goals | Pit stop | | |
| 15:30 | | | Pit stop | |
| 16:00 | Getting to know you | Inspiring ideas | Entrepreneurship panel | Cabaret preparation/ Facilitator final debrief |
| 17:00 | Reflections | Reflections | | Cabaret |
| 18:00 | Dinner | Dinner | Time to prepare | Awards and close |
| 19:00 | Time with Moi | Time with Moi | | Time with Moi |
| 19:30 | | | Networking with entrepreneurs | |
| 22:00 | Cultural awareness | Ethics | | Optional Gala dinner |

# Chapter 6

# Facilitators, Facilitation and the Administrative Team

Getting the most out of groups requires more than a clear agenda and relevant content. An integral component for the success of a programme like Enterprisers is the use of facilitators who help groups with both process and content. This chapter describes the facilitator model employed by the Enterprisers programme, presents conceptual frameworks for facilitation, and discusses the roles and responsibilities of the administrative support team.

## 6.1 Facilitative Leaders

The Enterprisers programme is fortunate to be "facilitator-rich", meaning that with a group of 64 participants, there are typically 2 lead facilitators and 16 group facilitators. The lead facilitators are responsible for coordinating the programme overall, including conducting the large-group sessions throughout the programme and meeting regularly with the group facilitators for training and review.

Each small group of eight participants works with a pair of facilitators during the 4-day programme. These facilitator pairs are members of the group, vested in the group and its goals, and serve as process and content experts. The facilitators believe that the team has all the wisdom, skills and knowledge it needs to improve itself. Facilitation creates a process that allows the team to improve with what they have.

## 6.2 Facilitative Model

Any programme needs to determine how it wants to use facilitators in the process. Enterprisers follows three underlying principles: (1) everyone is participating to learn together; (2) we operate in a "safe" environment, meaning that everyone feels safe to explore and discuss without judgement and (3) we create an environment in which participants can say and do things that stretch their imagination and self-confidence.

Participants are on a learning journey, focusing on five primary areas that affect their self-efficacy (Fig. 6.1).

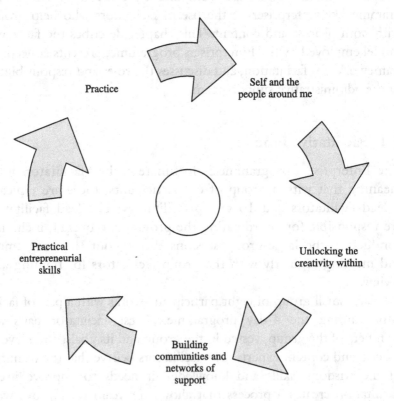

**Figure 6.1** Five components of the learning journey that affect participants' self-efficacy

## 6.3  Facilitator Criteria

Facilitation is a complex, challenging and multifaceted process and it is important to consider the criteria for selecting facilitators for any given programme. A programme designed for university students will require facilitators with certain skills, while a programme targeting corporate managers would need facilitators with other skills and abilities. While there is a broad discussion regarding facilitation techniques, we suggest that engaging participants, reflecting on group process, generating and sharing ideas and information are the most fundamental skills.

One model used to select facilitators for the Enterprisers programme considers four selection criteria: (1) minimal criteria, (2) desirables, (3) unacceptable qualities and (4) overall balance. We examine these with three levels of facilitators.

## 6.4  Lead Facilitators: Coordinating the Show

Every programme needs someone who is in charge and Enterprisers typically uses two individuals in the role of lead facilitator. These individuals coordinate and facilitate the overall flow of the 4-day programme, train the group facilitators and meet with them regularly during and throughout the programme, and conduct most of the large-group sessions. We suggest the following criteria for selecting the person(s) "in charge".

### 6.4.1  *Minimal Criteria*

It is critical that the lead facilitator buys into the vision and values of the programme and commits totally to the programme as it runs. Significant experience with interactive teaching is essential and there should be some element of entrepreneurship teaching and/or running a business or a growing organisation. Good communication and interpersonal skills are a must. Lead facilitators must be able to work as part of a team and they must be flexible, being able to flow easily and comfortably with unexpected changes that might happen. As the

Enterprisers programme continued, it also became a criterion that lead facilitators served as facilitators in one or more previous programmes.

### 6.4.2  *Desirables*

Beyond the minimal criteria described above, there are several qualities that are highly desirable for individuals in the lead facilitator roles. A high level of enthusiasm and a sense of humour top the list, followed by an ability to cope with challenges and a busy, intense week. Linking with the importance of being flexible, lead facilitators must be able to improvise and be at ease with public speaking. They must demonstrate good time keeping and have the ability to balance this timing with a sense of the moment, understanding what is happening around them at all times. The lead facilitators should also like networking and engaging with people, understand how to challenge others in a respectful way and be willing to listen.

### 6.4.3  *Unacceptable Attributes*

There are also warning signs to suggest individuals who should not be in the role of lead facilitator. On this list, they would be pessimism, not being open to learning and experimentation with new ideas, inappropriate criticism of colleagues and ideas, shutting people down, being ethnocentric, using inappropriate language, being late and being unprepared.

Whenever possible, it is useful to seek an overall balance between the two lead facilitators, considering experience of life, business and the universe, a gender balance and the entrepreneurial orientation of the individuals.

### 6.5  Facilitators

### 6.5.1  *What is Facilitation?*

There are numerous definitions of facilitation, but one that works successfully is that a facilitator is a person who helps a group improve the way it considers problems, solves them and makes decisions. The first task of a facilitator is as profoundly difficult as it is simple. It is to be there and say what you see. This needs to be done without making judgements. The second task is to create conditions that allow members of the team:

- To see the "whole" rather than just the "parts";
- To be willing to say what they know, think, feel and see (even in risky situations);
- To listen to others, even if they disagree with what they hear;
- To take wise decisions in their own (and the group's) best interest,
- To act responsibly and swiftly if actions are called for.

Facilitation is about the team learning, not the facilitator teaching. It is all about people discovering what they know — not being told what they don't.

We suggest four rules for effective facilitation:

1. The facilitator guides the team's working process. The key word is "guides".
2. The facilitator maximises the team's productivity by helping to minimise their "team process loss".
3. The facilitator supports the rigor of the team's thinking process.
4. The facilitator only does things for the team that its members cannot do for themselves in order for them to take responsibility for their own work.

Additionally, facilitators operate with a set of assumptions about the individuals in their group:

- Everybody does the best they can with what they have every minute. This includes the facilitator.
- Given the choice, people do what they are ready, willing and able to do.
- People change their behaviour when they gain new perceptions of what is possible. This happens if people can hear others'

perceptions and state their own without having to defend them — operating in a safe environment.

- We only move by moving. When people move around in workshops and meetings, they change the shape, flow, energy and possibilities in the room.

The implications of these four key assumptions are numerous. Facilitating groups, leaders and facilitators should:

- Design workshops and meetings in which people find it easy to move if they choose.
- Experiment with your capacity for tolerating statements you do not believe, ideas you oppose, or personal styles that make you uncomfortable.
- Learn to hear all views without reacting; the more you do this, the more the team is likely to express all sides of polarised issues.
- Listen for parts of each statement with which you agree. To the extent you act as if all statements contain value, the easier it becomes for the team to do the same.
- Assume some faulty assumptions, stereotyping, mistrust, and anxiety, and you will not be surprised or disappointed.
- Resist the tendency to manage anxiety by talking, asking questions, explaining, repeating, or changing the subject.
- Wait patiently — this is often all a team needs from the facilitator to shift towards active dialogue and creative collaboration.
- Allow team members to solve the team's problem.

During the early stages of the Enterprisers programme, facilitators typically came from the universities. Each university provided two facilitators from the faculty or staff of that institution and training and preparation occurred prior to the start of an Enterprisers programme. As the programme continued, a core group of facilitators became available and today facilitators are drawn from an ever-growing pool. These facilitators work in pairs and are the primary interface with the teams of eight participants during the programme.

## 6.5.2  Facilitators: Desired Qualities

### 6.5.2.1  Minimal criteria

Facilitators must buy into the vision and values of the programme and should have experience conducting interactive sessions at a student/executive level. They should have some element of entrepreneurship teaching and/or run a business. Good communication and interpersonal skills are essential and facilitators must be able to work as part of a team. They must also have the ability to be flexible.

### 6.5.2.2  Desirables

Like the lead facilitators, facilitators must also possess a sense of enthusiasm and a sense of humour. They should exude a positive attitude to life and have the talent to cope with an intense week full of challenges. Facilitators, because they work extensively with small groups, must enjoy networking and engaging with people, have the skills to challenge in a respectful way, and be cognizant of time keeping and being "in the moment".

### 6.5.2.3  Unacceptable attributes

Three unacceptable characteristics bear mention for facilitators: pessimism, not being open to learning and experimentation with new ideas and inappropriate criticism of colleagues and/or ideas.

Trying to achieve an overall balance among the facilitators, we look for experience of life, business and the universe, gender, sectoral expertise and entrepreneurial orientation. Given that the participants represent a broad spectrum of experiences and interests, it is useful to bring together facilitators representing a range of experiences and backgrounds.

## 6.5.3  Student Facilitators: Desired Qualities

As the Enterprisers programme continued being offered over time, we discovered that a number of participants were interested in becoming facilitators for future programmes. Clearly they had the valuable experience of going through the programme and, with proper training, they brought the talent and enthusiasm to serve effectively in this role. Over time, a pool of former participants who have served as facilitators has now developed and several of these individuals have graduated, started careers, and continue to come back as facilitators. Beyond the initial training for facilitators, it has proven most successful to pair a first-time facilitator (student or faculty) with an experienced facilitator whenever possible.

In considering a former participant for a facilitator position, we would look at the following criteria:

### 6.5.3.1 *Minimal criteria*

Similar to all facilitator categories, the former participant must buy into the vision and values of the programme. They must have participated fully in an Enterpriser programme and have a track record with taking and making a success of a project or business. Additionally, they must demonstrate strong communication and interpersonal skills and show the ability to work as part of a team. This group, too, must be flexible and able to flow with changes that might happen.

### 6.5.3.2 *Desirables*

It is helpful to have experience running interactive sessions at a student/executive level. Again, enthusiasm and a sense of humour go a long way towards positive facilitator behaviour. An ability to cope effectively with an intense week and with a variety of challenges is crucial and these student facilitators must also enjoy networking, engaging with people and having the ability to challenge others in a respectful way.

### 6.5.3.3 *Unacceptable attributes*

One characteristic unique to this group of facilitators is that they must avoid comments like "When I was at" — they cannot compare groups within the cohort or with past experiences. Like all facilitators, they must avoid pessimism, inappropriate criticisms of colleagues or ideas, and not being open to learning and experimentation with new ideas.

The overall balance we seek with the student facilitators includes their experience of life — the things they have done, gender balance, and an entrepreneurial orientation.

## 6.6 An Emphasis on Facilitation Skills

Every programme needs to consider the role of facilitators and these roles will vary. Let us suggest a few principles of facilitation that apply to nearly any setting.

First, a facilitator is a guide and it is the role of the facilitator to help individuals move through a process together, not to be the sage or font of knowledge. The facilitator is not there to give answers and opinion, but to draw out the opinions and ideas of group members.

Next, it is critical to recognise that facilitation emphasises how people participate in the process of learning, not just on what actually is accomplished or achieved. Frequently discussion focuses on the process the group went through more than on the end result.

Finally, facilitators are objective and neutral. It is not the function of the facilitator to take sides and, should this happen, it typically destroys the facilitator's ability to guide the team.

Facilitators use a variety of skills and techniques as they guide a group. It is important that the facilitators engage group members and reflect on the group process. This helps ensure that all group members have the opportunity to participate in the group process and to reflect on what happened. These skills emphasise the responsibility of each person as a member of the team.

## 6.7 Modes of Interactions

We present a model showing the modes of interactions within facilitated groups.[1] The model looks at the focus of the facilitator being on content or process and the attitude of the facilitator being more self-centred or group centred.

The self-centred, content orientation style indicates a domination mode, where the facilitator states "I know the right answer!" The self-centred, process orientation expresses a manipulation mode, with the facilitator telling the group to "Just follow my process!"

An effective facilitator is likely to be group centred. The group-centred, content approach leads to the inquiry mode, when facilitators ask "What might we learn from/about this?" And the fourth frame, the group-centred, process orientation sees the facilitator asking "How can I help you achieve your objectives?"

It is the facilitators' role to be process focused with the group or others in mind as opposed to being self-centred. This enables the facilitation process to help the group achieve their learning objectives.

| Manipulation | Facilitation |
|---|---|
| "Just follow my process!" | "How can I help you achieve your objectives?" |
| Domination | Teaching |
| "I know the right answer!" | "How can I support your learning?" |

**Figure 6.2** Modes of Interaction (courtesy of Hartmut Stuelten)

## 6.8 Styles of Facilitation

John Heron in his work *Helping the Client* suggested that there are six styles of managing and leading assigned to either a push or pull category.[2] We have found these useful as part of the training with facilitators in the Enterprisers programme.

A description of each style and some practical applications follow:

(1) Directing: Giving directions, advice and recommendations. This style uses the push approach. The directing style is useful if the participant lacks confidence, is unable to direct his/her own learning, or if there are legal, safety or ethical guidelines.

With each style, there are necessary skills to use and traps to avoid:

| Skills | Traps |
|---|---|
| Diagnosing learning needs | Giving unwanted advice |
| Insight into learning process | Taking over, imposing solutions |
| Giving clear instructions | Creating dependency |
| Explaining WHY | Hesitating when firmness needed |
| Motivating | Overcontrolling |

Examples:

- "Remember to include this information in your pitch."
- "Have you talked to your tutor about this?"
- "I suggest you attend this training course."

(2) Informing: Giving information and knowledge to the learner. This style uses the push approach and is used when the facilitator is showing where to find extra help or information, supplying missing facts, explaining what just happened or telling about your own experiences.

| Skills | Traps |
|---|---|
| Presenting information clearly | Overloading |
| Checking for understanding | Using too much jargon |
| Inviting and handling questions | Not saying WHY it's important |
| | TEACHING focus, not learning |

Examples:

- "You can find the information on this website."
- "If you need help, you can get it by pressing F1."
- "At my first presentation, I forgot to check the equipment."

(3) Confronting: Raising awareness; challenging assumptions. This style also represents the push orientation and is used to show consequences of a participant's actions, to challenge participants to

rethink assumptions, to raise awareness of others' perceptions and to boost the participant's confidence by affirming success.

| Skills | Traps |
| --- | --- |
| Direct questions | Avoiding painful issues |
| Giving constructive feedback | Acting like an angry parent |
| Challenging defensive excuses | Making character judgements |
| Giving room to reflect | Confronting on a trivial issue |
| | Creating win/lose outcomes |

Examples:

- "Are you aware that you are not using one of your key talents?"
- "We are running late because you could not reach a decision".
- "Are you assuming that it's the same problem as yesterday?"
- "You received very good comments about your last presentation".

(4) Supporting: Building the participant's self-esteem, self-confidence. This style moves the facilitator to the pull mode and is recommended to build morale and self-confidence, to encourage risk taking, and to reward success and promote further learning.

| Skills | Traps |
| --- | --- |
| Expressing appreciation | Patronising |
| Showing YOUR confidence | Giving "Yes, BUT". support |
| Sharing your mistakes | Overdoing it so it feels false |
| Encouraging SELF-respect | Held back by OWN inhibitions |
| Apologising when necessary | Sending mixed signals |

Examples:

- "I'm here all week if you need any more help."
- "You did a great job with the presentation."

- "I'm confident that you'll make a big success of it."
- "Don't worry if some of the details are missing at this stage."

(5) Releasing: Releasing emotions which block progress. Thus, pull style is used if the participant is afraid of risk or failure, if one feels incompetent, or if the participant is frustrated, demotivated or angry.

| Skills | Traps |
|---|---|
| Active listening | Talking, not listening |
| Questioning | Making it hard to express emotions |
| Showing empathy | Spending too long |
| Feeding back what you perceive | Going too deep |
| Creating a supportive climate | Sympathising too quickly |
| | Denying or criticising feelings |

Examples:

- "Why are you not very confident about this?"
- "What is the problem here?"
- "I have the impression that you don't agree with this."

(6) Enabling: Promoting self-discovery, self-directed learning. The third of the pull styles, enabling is used to achieve a deeper level of understanding, to encourage the participant to take responsibility, and to promote motivation and commitment.

| Skills | Traps |
|---|---|
| Wide range of questions | Too many closed questions |
| Reflecting and paraphrasing | Structuring too soon |
| Provoking curiosity | DIRECTING in other words |
| Keeping hands in pockets! | Following YOUR curiosity |
| Silence | Not clarifying objectives |

Examples:

- "What advice would you give to the next person to do this?"
- "How do you intend to start?"
- "What would you do differently next time?"
- "How important is this to you?"

Heron suggests that facilitators lead the group when they use the directive approaches of directing, informing or confronting and that they help the participants to lead when they use the supporting, releasing and enabling styles.

## 6.9  Stages of Group Development

Participants in a programme like Enterprisers are engaged in small and large groups and facilitators should also be familiar with stages of group development. Tuckman's work in this area is probably the most well-known, suggesting that groups progress through five stages: forming, storming, norming, performing and adjourning.[3]

During the forming stage, group members rely on safe, patterned behaviour and look to the facilitators for guidance and direction. Group members desire to be accepted by the group and need to know that the group is safe. It is typical that members gather impressions and information about the similarities and differences among them and form preferences for later subgroups or pairings.

The second stage, storming, is characterised by competition and conflict, sometimes in the personal-relations dimension and sometimes in the task-function dimension. As group members begin to organise for a task, conflict may arise in their personal relations. Individuals have to bend and mould their feelings, beliefs, attitudes and ideas to fit with the group. Communication is key in this stage: because of the conflict, some members may remain silent while others tend to dominate. Group members must move towards a problem-solving approach as they go to stage three. Facilitators must demonstrate excellent listening skills during this stage of group development.

Next is the norming stage, where interpersonal relations are characterised by cohesion. Here group members are engaged and recognise everyone's contributions, community building and the resolution of group issues. Leadership is typically shared when a group reaches the norming stage and trust develops. This is when individuals begin to appreciate a sense of group belonging. In the norming stage, group members share ideas and feelings, provide feedback to each other and explore actions related to the task. Creative thinking is generally high and there tends to be an opened and sharing of information on both a personal and task level.

Groups that reach stage four, the performing stage, display an interdependence in both personal relations and problem solving. Group members at stage four are both highly people oriented and highly task oriented. There is a strong sense of group identity and a genuine focus on problem solving.

The final stage, adjourning, involves the ending of task behaviours and, to a degree, disengagement from relationships that have formed. A planned ending usually includes recognition for participation and accomplishment and an opportunity for group members to say goodbye. The Enterprisers programme understands the importance of this fifth and final stage and concludes with individual and team recognition, including a final team presentation (the Cabaret), the awarding of individual certificates, and team photos sometimes followed by a celebratory dinner/party to end the programme.

## 6.10 Key Facilitation Skills

This chapter focuses on several skills and attributes important for effective facilitation. Facilitators must have a wide range of skills and techniques to be effective. For any programme using facilitators, selection and training are the keys. Excellent verbal and analytical skills are crucial. Facilitators must also know how to ask questions, when to ask them and how to 'push and pull' in different situations. Non-verbal communication skills are also important; facilitators should be keenly aware of the power of non-verbal behaviours such as eye contact, facial expressions, body language and posture/position and enthusiasm. Overall, a facilitator must be able to quickly read the group dynamics to guide the group effectively.

Numerous qualities and characteristics for successful facilitation have been covered in this chapter, but a summary of specific attributes would include the following:

- Genuine enthusiasm
- Active listening
- Openness
- Consistency
- Flexibility
- Clear focus — being there

While the facilitators are enormously important for the success of any programme, nothing would happen without a competent administrative team to handle the details.

## 6.11 Behind Every Successful Programme

### 6.11.1 *An Administrative Team*

Planning and preparation are the keys to the success of any programme and we will look at the approach of the Enterprisers programme as a guide for considering designing similar programmes for entrepreneurial learning. An important lesson learned is the value of having two administrative team members during the delivery of a programme. One person is frequently involved with behind-the-scenes work while the other is serving the public up front, from registering participants to answering questions to distributing materials.

As the Enterprisers programme has grown and developed over time, the responsibilities of the administrative team have increased. There is significant preplanning for a programme, followed by the actual implementation and delivery, and culminating in a variety of follow-up activities. The description of what happens with the various segments of the Enterprisers programme is provided to help others consider the details that must be covered for a programme to be a success.

### 6.11.2 *The Planning Stage*

Significant planning goes into making a programme a successful venture. Once dates have been chosen, a venue for the event must be selected. There are budget considerations, but of great importance is the venue itself. Our experience has shown that a location with accommodations, meeting rooms (sufficient for both large and small group sessions), and quality dining facilities on a campus or other location somewhat isolated from the surrounding town is an ideal setting. The administrative team identifies potential sites, negotiates expenses and hammers out the details about space, meals and other resources.

Once dates and locations have been selected, the administrative team coordinates the announcement of the programme and starts the application process for candidates. This involves working with various organisations and agencies and coordinating the application and selection process. Once candidates are selected, notification occurs and information about the programme is sent to selected participants. Information is also gathered from applicants, ranging from dietary restrictions to biographical background.

Manuals are prepared for participants and facilitators. These include descriptions of the activities and events for the 4-day programme along with all materials both participants and facilitators need. For programmes that will repeat, the goal is to design a manual that needs only minimal changes and updates as we move from one programme to the next.

The administrative team contacts facilitators for availability and makes arrangements for their accommodations and other needs. The training schedule is established so that facilitators meet prior to the programme to go over facilitation techniques and specific programme goals.

Materials are prepared and ordered and then packaged and sent to the programme venue. Because of very specific needs, it is critical that all materials are sent in advance or that the venue is able to provide what is required.

The administrative team is also involved in securing funding for the programme and for future programmes. Funding needs will vary with all types of programmes and could range from participant fees to external funding to grants. This is a continuous effort.

There are also outside guests who must be contacted for each programme. Examples include entrepreneurs who present as a part of the panel of entrepreneurs and a larger group of entrepreneurs who appear for the networking event. This must be done in a timely fashion so that a variety of entrepreneurial endeavours are represented during the programme.

### 6.11.3 *And So It Begins*

Organised chaos is a good description of what the opening of most programmes looks like, with eager participants arriving and a sense of both excitement and mystery in the air. It is the "organised" part of the chaos, however, that becomes crucial; it should not only look to everyone like everything is organised and under control, it also in fact should be that way. Here, again, is where the administrative team brings calm to the chaos.

The registration process should be set up and well organised long before the first participant arrives. Manuals, nametags, information, room assignments and other materials are arranged and easily distributed.

The large meeting room is set up with banners and sound systems for the lead facilitators to be able to begin the opening sessions. Facilitators can arrange their small-group meeting rooms so that they are ready to use for the initial team sessions on the first afternoon.

Photographs are taken of each participant so that they can add a "skills note" at the bottom and post the photo on a large skills board, giving everyone an opportunity to discover some insights about the other attendees.

Initial surveys or psychometric questionnaires can be distributed during the check-in process so that students can do a preassessment as they wait for the programme to officially begin. This is optimal for use by programme designers.

As the programme begins, the administrative team is available to assist the lead facilitators and facilitators with any needs. They are also constantly checking to make certain that equipment is delivered and functioning and that meals, coffee breaks, and other events are ready as scheduled. While coping with the daily routine, they are also busy preparing materials for upcoming sessions; for example, there is a lot of preparation for the networking event with 20–30 visiting entrepreneurs.

The core duties of the administration team would include the following:

Gathering the funding from sponsors, government agencies and individuals. This needs to be sufficient to cover each event and to have some surplus left over to fund the annual running costs of the team.

Budget estimates full economic costing. To raise such funding and to ensure that Enterprisers is self-sustaining, annual budgets have to be planned to include salaries, institutional overheads, hospitality costs, professional fees, consumables, marketing, printing, travel and hospitality.

Marketing and recruitment of facilitators and students is perhaps the most time-consuming part of the activity. Marketing and communication needs to include the use of the website, print materials, e-mails, referrals and an entire suite of activities that needs to engage the imagination of a professional marketing colleague. The cautionary note is that Enterprisers needs to be run in a particular style of informality (but with depth) and the marketing colleague needs to be able to tune into this. The administrators may well have to do some hard negotiation with the institution on the level of flexibility available to them. Not to mention the usual discussions about who has sign-off on branding and PR.

Ensuring attendance of students, especially if they are not paying fees is crucial to the success of the programme. We have found that there is great enthusiasm at the start of the process, but as time approaches to head off for 4 days, a few people begin to find other priorities! This is mainly because the message about benefits is best acquired on the course and almost no amount of marketing can be the same as the actual participative experience. So, the method we have used is to secure a "refundable" deposit, where so long as the delegate attends the whole programme they receive their deposit back in full.

Securing facilitators is central to the success of the programme. These are the individuals who give up 4 days of their time (plus another 2 days for training) and only have their expenses reimbursed.

So, this is a major time commitment and because their motives are mainly altruistic, it would seem harsh to impose "quality control". But this is essential to the success. The selection criteria have already been in place. It only remains that the administration needs to ensure timely information, transparent procedures and an entirely professional management of the facilitators so that their experience is also excellent.

Networking event requires a lot of effort to gather some 20 entrepreneurs and business advisors from the local region. These people need to be informative, open and understand that they play two roles; educative and informational. They too need careful management.

The team needs to prepare mini-biographies, badges, arrange parking where required, send out accurate information of the event, logistics as well as a briefing note. Personal contacts and prior connections are most helpful. Imagination is needed to ensure that the guests have a close fit with the needs of the students.

We have used 8-foot-tall bamboos (garden) poles on which we have tied laminated flags that have the names of the guests so that it is easier for the students to find the people they want.

Some duplication of skills, knowledge and information is good — in case one or two drop out on the night.

Beyond this — standard networking event management principles apply — that the hospitality is good, atmosphere friendly and that the venue is suitable so that the din that starts up with 80+ people in a room can dissipate.

Materials. There is a large amount of consumables required.

Flip charts; post it notes; colour felt tip pens, white board pens, blue tack, bits of card board, tubes from kitchen roll, tapes, etc., for each breakout area as well as for the main room.

Video camera, digital camera if possible a Polaroid, for the wall of fame. Use these as much as possible to capture images that can be used later for social network sites, marketing, etc.

Also have some fun materials around such as giant jenga, and so forth to create "play" facilities during break times. Social interaction time can never be underestimated as a means of bonding and allowing people time to create further opportunities and conversations.

Event management should be based on well-recognised project management schedules, perhaps computer software and very regular updates by the implementation team. This programme requires a lot of aggregation of information, materials, etc., and it is easy to leave something out and even a small omission can spoil the flow of the programme.

Joining instructions, informing people about deposits, where to come and links to any surveys need to be prepared well in advance and sent out to people as soon as they are confirmed. This ensures deeper buy-in. The more this can be managed via the internet the better.

Certification is much favoured by delegates and this can be preprared for each person as they sign up so that the whole thing is ready for distribution at the ceremony on the last day.

Style of the event — creating the right atmosphere is also an important element. And there are a number of factors that come into play. The delivery team must be and must seem to be organised, happy and enjoying the event. Negative vibes of any disorganisation can seriously damage the atmosphere.

Further, there needs to be a feeling of a safe environment and sometimes a "silly" environment just so that people relax enough to learn. Music is an important component, and here — the project needs a PA system, music (MP3 player) as intro and outro to each session and a sense of fun.

Sponsors need to be found wherever possible to reduce the costs of the event and hence the liability for each institution. The event already secures a huge level of unrecognised sponsorship in the form of volunteer time from the facilitators. Annual cycles of securing sponsorship is really important. A typical end of course dinner is the best offer as this usually has a great atmosphere and VIPs can be invited to join them.

Powerpoints that are used in the programme can be made available on request.

PA system that can handle two microphones and music is an essential equipment. Not all venues are well equipped and if the intention is to run several programmes per year — it is best to buy a good-quality system.

Name badges to be prepared — but only with the first name. Try and get badges that are easy to use and that students can attach to collars, etc., so that they are visible during the programme.

Skills wall is a way for delegates to stick a Polaroid picture of with a post-it note to describe themselves. This is quite useful during the programme for two main reasons. The first is that the registration team at the desk get to look each delegate in the eye and hence start to get to know them and secondly the pictures and post-it notes are used during break times to get an overview of who is around and what skills there are in the gathering.

Hospitality is very important. Almost everyone has come for free, given their time for free and so there needs to be the right level of hospitality that recognises goodwill and gives back.

Professionalism of the admin team is, of course, to be expected. It is quite important when this team is put in place that there is one very experienced person — in terms of event management skills, together with an eye for detail.

## 6.12 After the Programme

### 6.12.1 *The Work Continues*

Following four intense days — five or six for the facilitators and administrative crew — there is little time to relax before follow-up ensues. The administrative team promotes an on-going website to build a network of Enterprisers and does an evaluation of the programme, including tabulating the surveys of participants. These are the more mundane, but certainly important tasks, like preparing travel expense reimbursements for the facilitators. And with little delay, the administrative team begins planning for the next Enterprisers, including seeking funding, finding venues and starting the application process and call for facilitators.

What does one look for in the administrative team? Certainly the team must have a penchant for details and be exceptionally organised. They need to possess the ability to deal successfully with stress and to remain calm and confident in the midst of chaos. Strong communication and interpersonal skills are essential and a sense of humour is a must. The administrative team must also be able to function effectively as members of the team, working comfortably with the lead facilitators, facilitators and the participants.

## 6.13 Lessons Learned

This chapter provides descriptions of facilitation and of the roles and responsibilities of the lead facilitators, facilitators and administrative team. We have learned from our experiences that it is important for the lead facilitators and the facilitators to form trusting pairs and to provide a combination of warmth and wisdom. Credibility must be quickly gained and at the same time participants need to feel comfortable. Facilitators must be able to be challenging and also guide participants through finding creative solutions.

The administrative team creates an environment where the lead facilitators and facilitators can do their work comfortably and without interruption, knowing that all of the behind-the-scenes details are well organised and clearly executed.

The selection, training and team development of the facilitators and administrative team are absolutely essential for creating an environment that is conducive to accomplishing the goals and objectives of a programme like Enterprisers.

## Endnotes

1. Modes of Interaction, Hartmurt Stuelten, Ashridge Consulting.
2. John Hiron, Complete Facilitators Handbook (1999).
3. Bruce W. Tuckman, Mary Ann C. Jensen (1977). Stages of Small-Group Development Revisited. *Group Organisation Management*, 2(4), 419–427.

Chapter 7

# Evaluating Enterprisers: A Look at Findings about Self-Efficacy

The Cambridge–MIT Institute (CMI) was developed as part of a major effort to enhance levels of innovation and entrepreneurship and focused on the examination of deep personal values and the underlying motivations of individuals with entrepreneurial potential. The content of the initial *CMI-Connections* programme was developed with a belief that the enhancement of individual self-confidence played a significant role in starting new enterprises. As the programme has evolved into the current *Enterprisers* model, this notion of building one's self-confidence remains an integral part of the content design.

Three forms of measurement and evaluation have been used consistently with each *Connections* and *Enterprisers* programme. The first, which will only be mentioned in this chapter, is a standard evaluation of the individual components of the programme along with questions regarding the venue, meals and accommodations. The instrument asks participants to rate each component of the overall programme on a 1–5 scale and asks for feedback in open-ended questions about the overall value of the programme, suggestions for changes, and comments on the venue.

The second is to acknowledge the growth and development of the programme in terms of reach and general impact. Two graphs are presented here to illustrate the point.

Since its inception, there have been just over a 1000 students (to date) who have participated. These include undergraduates in the early years, changing to postgraduates in more recent programmes and also 54 faculty of Portsmouth University — who have since run their own programmes.

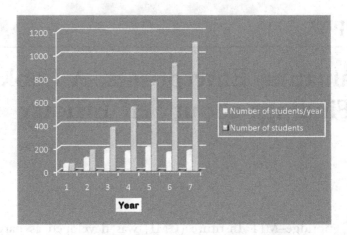

**Figure 7.1**   Growth of Student Numbers

There has been a multiplier effect because staff of a number of universities have also taken either whole or parts of Enterprisers and used them in their own institutions. By way of illustration the pie chart below indicates the breadth of coverage of the delegates over the 20 programmes.

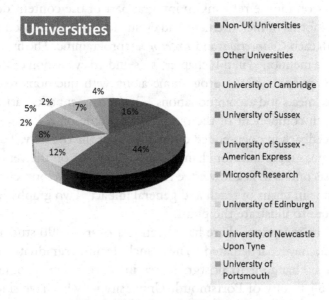

**Figure 7.2**   Spread of Participation

This chapter focuses on work that has been ongoing concerning enhancing self-efficacy to enable entrepreneurship. William Lucas at MIT and Sarah Cooper at the University of Strathclyde have conducted research with participants in the *Connections* and *Enterprisers* programmes from the beginning, using a pre-programme questionnaire, a post-programme questionnaire, and a follow-up survey 6 months after participating in the programme.

One of the most significant findings is that *Connections* and *Enterprisers* have created sustained improvements in entrepreneurial self-efficacy, along with a related strengthening of pre-entrepreneurial awareness and exploration of ideas for starting companies.[1]

## 7.1 Entrepreneurship in a Changing World

Interest in new venture creation and entrepreneurship generally has received increased attention worldwide. Some countries have struggled with how to change negative perceptions of entrepreneurship into a more positive image, while other countries such as China have seen significant cultural shifts towards supporting entrepreneurial endeavours.

Economic factors have also gone through deep and dramatic changes. Beginning in 2007 and continuing through today, many large companies have downsized, restructured, or, in certain cases, closed completely. While the recent economic recession has been difficult for many, it has also created opportunities for entrepreneurs.

## 7.2 The Development of Self-efficacy

One of the primary goals of entrepreneurship education at colleges and universities around the world has been to promote entrepreneurship as a career choice, helping individuals to change perceptions about success and failure and to shatter beliefs that entrepreneurship is a shady occupation. Questions have consistently been raised regarding the qualities necessary for becoming a successful entrepreneur and, while there is typically a long list of characteristics identified, there is no universal agreement on what these qualities are or should be.

One characteristic that does stand out among the crowd is confidence. An individual or team must have a sense of self-belief in their ability to start a new venture. It is this quality of self-efficacy that is critical to a person's willingness to find opportunities and begin entrepreneurial endeavours. Discovering opportunities and engaging in entrepreneurial behaviour have been linked with high-levels of self-efficacy.[2] And Bandura[3] considered that self-efficacy beliefs are imbedded in people's understanding of their abilities to implement certain actions to produce certain results and that people's motivations are frequently based more on their self-beliefs than what may be actually true.

Bandura's social cognitive theory focuses on the concept of self-efficacy and emphasises three factors in the development of personality: observational learning, social experience, and reciprocal determinism. Bandura believes that an individual's self-system is determined by their attitudes, abilities and cognitive skills. Simply stated, Bandura views self-efficacy as a person's belief in his or her ability to succeed in a specific situation.

Most people are able to identify goals and objectives they want to achieve, change or accomplish. It is the action involved to bring about these achievements, changes or accomplishments that factor into an individual's self-efficacy. Bandura[4] suggests that individuals approach these tasks in quite different ways depending on their level of self-efficacy.

Bandura suggests that people with a high level of self-efficacy:

- View challenging problems as situations to be mastered;
- Develop stronger interest in the activities in which they become involved;
- Create a deeper sense of commitment to their activities and interests;
- Recover rapidly from setbacks.

People with a lower level of self-efficacy:

- Think that challenging tasks are beyond their abilities;
- Avoid difficult tasks;

- Lose confidence in their personal abilities;
- Emphasise negative outcomes and personal failures.[2]

## 7.3 Bandura's Sources of Self-Efficacy

Self-efficacy develops through a wide variety of experiences, tasks and situations. As people continue to develop new skills, experiences, and understanding, self-efficacy continues to grow.

According to Bandura, there are four distinct sources of self-efficacy. The first is through what he describes as mastery experiences, suggesting that one's self-efficacy is strengthened by performing a task successfully. Self-mastery is accomplished even when people succeed at performing some portions of a task. Some of the exercises and activities included in the Enterprisers programme help participants to experience success in small steps before moving them to more challenging and complex tasks. Successes are celebrated in small and large groups throughout the programme.

The second source is described as social modelling. Social modelling involved the observation of others successfully completing a task or reaching a goal. These observations may lead the observer to believe that they, too, have the ability to succeed with such a task. Facilitators often are viewed as role models for participants in Enterprisers. They promote the development of new skills and new learning and encourage participants as they tackle new challenges.

A third source of self-efficacy is labelled as Social Persuasion. This is one of the sources that is most pronounced during the Enterprisers program. It is the concept that individuals could be persuaded to believe that they do have the abilities and skills to succeed. Verbal encouragement from facilitators and colleagues can help an individual to believe they can accomplish a particular task. Facilitators frequently offer encouragement and praise as they see improvement in particular skills.

The final source of self-efficacy that Bandura identifies is what he calls Psychological Responses. Bandura (1994) believes that an individual's moods, emotions, stress levels, and physical reactions can all affect how someone feels about their abilities in a specific situation.

He continues that by learning how to deal with minimizing stress or working with moods when facing challenging situations, individuals can improve their level of self-efficacy.

Facilitators perform a number of functions during the Enterprisers program. At various levels, facilitators participate, demonstrate, coach, mentor, inspire, and congratulate. These roles allow the participants to experience several of the sources of self-efficacy: enactive self-mastery, role modelling and verbal persuasion and these lead to increased self-efficacy and performance/accomplishment.

There is a fine balance between one's sense of self and the accuracy of that self-image. Someone with an unrealistic image of their skills and abilities may well put themselves in a position to fail and, likewise, someone with a lower self-image may not push themselves to reach what they are capable of doing. One of the principles of Enterprisers is to stretch the participants in one or more areas of development, believing that stretching a person will further develop their self-efficacy. One simple, yet striking, example of this was a participant in an Enterprisers programme who had never spoken in front of a group and was terrified of doing so; on the final day of the programme, she volunteered to do her group's pitch in front of 80 people.

An important lesson learned from the Enterprisers experiment is that entrepreneurship education in whatever form must develop the self-efficacy and confidence of participants.

It is important here to distinguish between self-efficacy, self-confidence and self-esteem. Self-efficacy is typically aligned with specific tasks or goals whereas self-confidence is viewed more as a personality trait that generally assumes a level of confidence in most situations. Self-esteem is widely viewed as to how much an individual likes himself or herself. This has significant implications for both the content and the teaching. The Enterprisers programme has been developed to provide high levels of experiential and reflective learning.

Rae and Carswell[5] have indicated that entrepreneurial self-efficacy can be enhanced through teaching methods which encourage participants to learn through the experience of others, as well as through their own endeavours and approaches. One of the strategies employed by the Enterprisers programme is to bring in entrepreneurs for a panel discussion focusing on successes and failures and to provide a networking event with a significant number of entrepreneurs where participants have opportunities for one-to-one discussions.

The Enterprisers programme consists of a variety of individual, small- and large-group activities that overall help the development of self-efficacy along with other skills important for the potential entrepreneur. The programme strives to bring together participants from different cultures and backgrounds and emphasises a number of skills around developing and working with effective teams.

## 7.4 Can Teaching Cultivate Self-Efficacy?

Bandura[2] stated that during the formative period of children's lives, schools function as the primary environment for the cultivation and development of cognitive competencies. Schools are where children acquire knowledge and learn problem-solving skills and the task of creating these environments rests mainly on the capabilities and self-efficacy of teachers. Teachers also tend to operate collectively rather than as individuals within a school system and the culture of that system can have positive or negative effects on how effectively schools function as a social system.

School systems have tried a variety of educational approaches through the years and some of these have actually led to lower self-efficacy. Some of these approaches include a lock-step curriculum that may lose students along the way or grouping students by ability, frequently lowering the self-efficacy of students placed in low-ability classes.

The Enterprisers programme focuses on both collaborative learning and personal improvement and development. Competition is rarely included; every participant has something to offer to the larger group.

## 7.5 A Reflective Moment

### 7.5.1 *The Enterprisers Curriculum and Delivery*

Enterprisers focuses on key themes which help participants pursue the new enterprise development process and support participants in the development of new business, social enterprise and not-for-profit initiatives. Each day has a specific focus:

Day One: *Moi.* The first day emphasises understanding one's self and personal motivations, goals, values and ethics.

Day Two: *Ideation.* The programme focuses during the second day on helping participants to understand what an entrepreneur is, the creative process and where ideas come from.

Day Three: *Nuts'n'Bolts.* The third day explores what it takes to succeed, looking at issues around leadership, building teams, and the acquisition of resources.

Day Four: *Crystal Ball.* The final day looks at how participants can maintain motivation and sustain ideas and projects.

The content of Enterprisers is delivered using a variety of teaching methodologies to create a mix of learning strategies and possibilities. Large-group sessions are used to deliver core sessions of the programme and participants are split into smaller sessions led by facilitators for more highly engaging and participative activities and exercises. The programme exposes participants to guest entrepreneurs and introduces concepts important for planning, networking and obtaining resources.

## 7.6  The Enterprisers' "Can Do" Attitude

### 7.6.1  *And Self-Efficacy*

One of the primary underlying assumptions of the Enterprisers programme is that individuals do have an entrepreneurial spirit, a "can do" attitude. The programme engages directly and indirectly with the development of self-efficacy by challenging assumptions, creating opportunities to try new things, establishing situations where individuals can observe how others do things, and by providing venues to acquire new knowledge.

It has been established that self-efficacy typically pertains to particular tasks, so people may have high self-efficacy for certain tasks and low self-efficacy for others. People with a high level of self-efficacy tend to work hard and continue even when faced with failure. One of the areas of interest is that people with high self-efficacy generally receive feedback from others in a positive fashion and view constructive feedback as useful. Specific, relevant and timely feedback is provided throughout the Enterprisers programme and is viewed as a means to help develop participants' self-efficacy.

## 7.7 Measuring Self-Efficacy

### 7.7.1 *The Methodology*

As mentioned earlier, two colleagues from the Cambridge–MIT Initiative, William Lucas and Sarah Cooper, have been assessing the impact of Enterprisers since the beginning. Data were collected on two proximate measures of the programme's effectiveness, and a third metric followed-up on the effect of the programme on participants 6 months following their participation in the programme. The assessment of self-efficacy used a pretest before the programme started and two post-tests, one at the end of the programme and one that followed 6 months later. It was determined that a pre- and post-test were required to measure if any change occurred during and because of the programme. An abbreviated postassessment was given during the last day of the programme to determine the amount of change that could be based on the Enterprisers programme; a second postassessment was administered 6 months later to measure if any enduring change remained after the programme's initial enthusiasm had diminished.

The assessment measures focused mainly on estimating the participants' sense of personal competency in both general skills and in their understanding of and capacity to undertake entrepreneurship; asked questions about their envisioned career and sought the frequency of behaviours believed to be precursors of entrepreneurship.[6]

Lucas and Cooper considered three questions regarding pre-entrepreneurial behaviours of the participants in Enterprisers. They ask how often individuals talk about ideas for starting new ventures, whether they return to talk about those ideas again, and whether they actually take steps to look into actual possibilities for starting the venture.

Results from Enterprisers indicate that the programme does have a significant impact on the self-efficacy of participants. Results show that after the 4-day programme there were increases in reported self-efficacy across all areas, with changes ranging from small to major increases.

The following two tables show the results from pre-event to post-event (Table 7.1) and from preevent to after 6 months (Table 7.2). These results are specifically from the participants attending the 2003 programme held at the University of Strathclyde, but it should be noted that the results of subsequent programmes continue to show similar trends.

Table 7.1   Pre- to Post-Event Changes in Levels of Self-Efficacy

| A. Self-efficacy: Current skill levels compared to university students | Percent ranking their skill "Good" to "Excellent" | |
| --- | --- | --- |
| N = 55 students | Pre-event | Postevent |
| Design something novel | 57.4% | 85.5% |
| Solve an unstructured problem | 74.1% | 85.5% |
| Clearly describe a problem orally | 51.9% | 72.7% |
| Clearly describe a problem in writing | 63.0% | 72.2% |
| Ask probing questions that clarify facts | 51.9% | 83.6% |
| Recognise a good opportunity | 66.7% | 83.6% |
| Motivate others to work together | 59.3% | 70.9% |
| Understand what it takes to start your own business | 24.1% | 72.7% |
| Start a successful business if you want | 20.4% | 67.3% |
| B. Envisioned work situations by time Periods (immediately, within 5 years 5 to 10 years, more than 10, or Never) | Percent seeing themselves in situation within 5 years | |
| In new venture (owned by others) | 70.8% | 64.6% |
| As business owner (employing others) | 27.6% | 44.7% |
| Self-employed (working for self) | 29.2% | 41.7% |

*Modified from* Lucas and Cooper (2004). "Enhancing self-efficacy to enable entrepreneurship: the case of CMI's Connections", Paper presented to High-Technology Small Firms Conference at the 12th Annual International Conference at the University of Twente, Enschede, The Netherlands.

Table 7.2    Pre- to After 6 Months Changes in Levels of Self-Efficacy

| A. Self-efficacy: Current skill levels compared to university students | Percent ranking their skill "Good" to "Excellent" | |
|---|---|---|
| Response rate at post-test, 50.9%, for $N = 28$ | Pre-event | After 6 months |
| Design something novel and innovative | 44.4% | 66.7% |
| Solve an unstructured problem | 74.1% | 77.8% |
| Clearly describe a problem orally | 51.9% | 85.2% |
| Clearly describe a problem in writing | 66.7% | 77.8% |
| Ask probing questions that clarify facts | 61.5% | 80.8% |
| Recognise a good opportunity | 70.4% | 74.1% |
| Motivate others to work together | 59.3% | 74.1% |
| Understand what it takes to start your own business | 19.2% | 76.9% |
| Start a successful business if you want | 22.2% | 59.3% |
| **B. Envisioned work situations by time Periods (immediately, within 5 years, 5 to 10 years, more than 10, or never)** | **Percent seeing themselves in situation in 5 years** | |
| In new venture (owned by others) | 63.0% | 40.7% |
| As business owner (employing others) | 17.9% | 28.6% |
| Self-employed (working for self) | 17.9% | 21.4% |

*Modified from* Lucas and Cooper (2004). Enhancing self-efficacy to enable entrepreneurship: the case of CMI's Connections. Paper presented to High-Technology Small Firms Conference at the 12th Annual International Conference at the University of Twente, Enschede, The Netherlands.

The most interesting findings from this study show that self-efficacy increased in every area after participating in the intensive 4-day programme. It is important to note that many ratings found in the pre-event category are relatively high, suggesting that individuals who were initially attracted to the programme brought some entrepreneurial skills with them.

The on-going experience of the Enterprisers programme indicates similar findings. The backgrounds of participants have changed with Enterprisers moving from working primarily with undergraduate university students to PhD students in engineering and technology and the social sciences. While the pre-event ratings may shift to some degree, there continues to be an increase in self-efficacy across areas following the 4-day intensive experience.

Table 7.2 examines the levels of self-efficacy from pre-event to 6 months following the programme. The total number of respondents to the follow-up survey was one-half of the original total, so there will be some differences in the pre-event percentage ranking their skill "good to excellent" from the data shown in Table 7.1.

Results from the survey 6 months following the programme indicate that participants continued to demonstrate strong levels of self-efficacy, specifically around skills of motivating others, understanding what is involved in starting a company, and displaying confidence that they could start a company if they wanted to so. Participants in the programme also showed increased confidence levels in communication skills, especially in their written and oral communication skills used in problem-solving situations.

It should be noted that there were some decreases in levels of self-efficacy from immediately after the programme to 6 months later, but even in these cases there was still an increase overall from the pre-event ratings to those reported 6 months after the event.

One of the questions posed in the work by Lucas and Cooper is whether the nature and scale of ambition was altered as a result of the programme. They believe that the programme had not succeeded in shifting people towards a "high growth entrepreneurship" agenda and recommended changes in the curriculum to reflect this goal. However, the recommendation comes in the light of the original funding from the Cambridge–MIT Institute. Since the funding sources changed — the overall aims of the programme also changed to include transferable (creative) skills, the training of doctoral candidates in commercialisation, creating social capital, a greater emphasis on social ventures and opening up people to the vast array of possibilities. The programme also became a training ground for educators to learn new skills and techniques in educating through "learning by doing" methods.

This is not to deny the need for ambitious thinking in the programme (hence the strap line — what are you waiting for?) but only to acknowledge that there are many objectives and each organising team/institution will need to decide on their priorities and adjust the measurement metrics accordingly.

## 7.8 Lessons Learned

What has been learned from the experience of running numerous programmes? The camaraderie, energy and positive spirit of the participants are palpable. The on-going research conducted by William Lucas and Sarah Cooper provides evidence that this kind of intensive experience enhances the development of entrepreneurial skills.

One of the key lessons learned concerns the importance of learning by doing. This has been an essential component of the Enterprisers concept since the beginning. An intensive experience with numerous structured interventions provides this opportunity. It is interesting to note that various institutions of higher education are today integrating this concept of action learning into the curriculum.

Finally, a noteworthy lesson from the research is recognising how critical it is to develop individual self-confidence — a belief that one can do something new and different — as a fundamental factor towards developing entrepreneurial skills.

What follows in the next chapter, demonstrates most clearly the effects of Enterprisers — stories from participants and facilitators regarding ideas and accomplishments.

### Endnotes

1. W. A. Lucas and S. Y. Cooper (2004). "Enhancing self-efficacy to enable entrepreneurship: the case of CMI's Connections", Paper presented to High-Technology Small Firms Conference at the 12th Annual International Conference at the University of Twente, Enschede, The Netherlands.
2. A. Ardichvili, R. Cardozo and S. Ray (2003). "A theory of entrepreneurial opportunity identification and development", *Journal of Business Venturing*, 18, pp. 105–123.

3. A. Bandura (1994). *Self-efficacy.* In V. V. Ramachaudran (Ed.) Encyclopedia of Human Behavior, 4. New York: Academic Press, pp. 71–81.
4. A. Bandura (1997). *Self-Efficacy: The Exercise of Control,* New York, Freeman.
5. D. Rae and M. Carswell (2000). "Using a life-story approach in researching entrepreneurial learning: the development of a conceptual model and its implications in the design of learning experiences", *Education + Training,* 42, 4/5, pp. 220–227.

# Chapter 8

# Cases and Speechless Moments!

We are often asked what difference Enterprisers make to those who attend. One form of response is naturally the quantitative indicators. Measuring and understanding the impact of education is really quite hard. Finding the causal links between what happened on the course, which elements made a difference and how to attribute the changes directly to the educational experience are all subject to much research.

We have chosen to report the impact of Enterprisers in two main ways. The first, based on a longitudinal study on measuring entrepreneurial intent was reported in Chapter 7.

In this chapter, we would like to highlight a few case studies that have inspired us to believe not only the numbers, the stats, but in the power of individual stories that have made the direct links from education to the outcomes.

We also have two unique contributions from the Universities of Sussex and Newcastle in terms of how the train the trainer model — conducted real time on the programme itself subsequently inspired whole new generations of enterprise education.

There are several layers at which individual stories inform us about expecting the unexpected from the work we do. In some ways the stories also somewhat challenge the notion of luck in entrepreneurship and instead reinforce the fact that if you want to make a difference you need to be among people who are also similarly minded and be open to conversations, ideas and be an active listener to see opportunities and pluck them from their low-hanging branches.

So, whether you skim read this section or choose to drill into the effects and processes described we hope you to get inspired to think of enterprise education differently.

## 8.1  Dr Sunny Kotecha — Participant and Facilitator

Sunny was in her last year at Oxford University, completing her PhD in Education at Nuffield College, when she was reflecting on the next stages in her career. In part, Sunny was somewhat confused and frustrated to identify what she should do next. Just at that time, she came across the publicity for Enterprisers and decided to apply for it, on the basis that it would give her a chance to mingle with others at similar stages of their career as herself and give her some time out to think. She was also looking for sources of inspiration for her next moves and the possibility of a fresh outlook.

Here is what Sunny got in terms of outcomes:

"I was able to meet new people in related fields, like-minded other students from other universities, including MIT, Cambridge and elsewhere. I was also able to meet people from corporates such as American Express and Microsoft and to interact with experienced facilitators and leaders from business. One of my main sources of inspiration was listening to the real-life examples; the entrepreneurs who present their stories at the panel discussion on entrepreneurship.

My real inspiration came in absorbing the eye-opening "can-do" attitude of Enterprisers — a huge change from the academic world I had so far inhabited.

It was during such a panel discussion that I came up with my business idea and was inspired to realise my desire to be an entrepreneur. The name for my company "Silver Lining Coaching", sprang from the stories I heard during this time. Not only was the inspiration for the name and the confirmation of intent shaped on Enterprisers, but the first client was also secured at the course, during the gala dinner. I have since expanded the business and am now working internationally with universities in the United States and individuals from many "blue-chip" organisations.

As a regular facilitator on Enterprisers, I keep fresh and energised. It is also a source of inspiration, as mingling and networking with people from such diverse backgrounds gives me a chance to try out some of my new ideas for the market! In addition, the chance to meet and hear from other entrepreneurs allows me to see business skills and decisions from different angles — a truly rare opportunity."

Sunny captures the community spirit of the programme. Having got something from it — she is ready to give back. The programme delegates benefit from her regular participation as a facilitator and real-life example.

Silver Lining Coaching provides communications training and coaching to a variety of corporate and community clients (www. silverliningcoaching.com). The company's unique strength is the ability to focus on what can be done rather than what cannot. Many organisations and courses aim to "fix" people whilst encouraging an emphasis on weaknesses. At Silver Lining, they apply the scientific research that shows using a positive focus leads to much better — and sustainable — results.

The most genuinely exciting part of Silver Lining's business is the ability to open people's eyes to how they can improve their productivity every day — not just after a 6-month review, or for a few days after having attended a course. For example, Silver Lining Coaching presented at the annual Centre for Applied Positive Psychology (CAPP) conference at Warwick University on "Positive Body Language for Everyday Use" and the audience were astounded to see the real and applicable uses for the positive psychology theories which so far have mostly been consigned just to books and papers.

At this point, Silver Lining Coaching has been in operation for almost 2 years, with clients ranging from Microsoft to local government and carrying out pro-bono work for student charities.

## 8.2 Skeleton Productions

Having evolved out of a university business school itself it is not surprising that Nottingham-University-based Skeleton Productions have chosen to send all three of their directors on Enterprisers. Annual visits enable them to tap into all the latest entrepreneurial thinking, grill the major figures and network with successful business people from all over the United Kingdom. A bit like an enterprising health check but without any costs!

Having first attended Enterprisers when working from their bedrooms health check Jonathan English (and twice Enterprisers attendee) says the Enterprisers experience has been a major part in pushing them to success.

> "Attending Enterprisers re-energises you when you may be having doubts, gives you new ideas when feeling stagnant and refuels you with the belief that you can succeed in your aspirations. Being able to chat day in day out to Cambridge Professors as well as take on the brightest MIT can offer at Connect 4 is an incredible opportunity, as Mastercard's advertising guru's would say some things are just priceless!"

Since January 2008 Skeleton has evolved into a well established *online video production company specialising in high-quality low-cost videos for the web*, a massively growing area in Europe and especially across the pond in America. Jonathan acknowledges having always had a personal love of technology but confesses:

> "Operating in the creative industries it's easy to forget about the importance of technology. The hi-tech nature of many of those at Enterprisers demands you to constantly ask how can we innovate? How can we improve? How can we use technology to make our business more effective and profitable?"

This constant questioning evolved into a process within Skeleton of continually asking how could we do things differently, less labour intensively and more profitably. This in itself led to one of the company's most important innovations; the building of a nationwide freelance network of film-makers. Instead of carrying the burden of expensive in-house teams Skeleton now have an army of freelance film-makers working for them all over the United Kingdom, enabling them to offer high-quality, low-cost video at 48 hours notice anywhere in the country.

## 8.3 Katie Hart — Participant and Facilitator

Enterprisers has spurred me on massively — having been involved in so many programmes I have lost count! I am now running a social project called Curb Your Consumption (http://www.curbyourconsumption.co.uk) which aims to work with consumers to generate ideas about how we can reduce over-consumption patterns in United Kingdom in favour of more sustainable alternatives.

## 8.4 Jesse Costelloe — Australia

I am unsure how to begin a reflection except perhaps to look in a mirror. The mirror I stumbled across branded Enterprisers washed up upon the golden beaches of the exquisite Sunshine Coast in Queensland Australia in mid-2007.

I'm 23, like music, some sports, clothes, movies, books, cooking, creating, connecting, humanity and if they will allow me to speak on behalf of all "enterprisers" have a desire to better myself and the world in which I inhabit through creative endeavours wrapped in a pastry called entrepreneurship.

My initial enrolment into university was driven by a desire to connect with like-minded individuals and further develop my skill sets so that I could further develop my own creative outlet; a technology and furniture design, manufacture and distribution business called Evok.

Unfortunately I found that with conventional academia came a conventional mindset. Most other students and a lot of academics within my university did not share any of the desires or passions that lay at the core of my individuality.

As a very frustrated and disheartened student, I approached my university and voiced my concerns and was thankfully offered a place on the 4-day Enterprisers programme. I can say from the bottom of my heart that this was one of the most inspiring passionate motivational experiences of my life and made my time at university worthwhile.

Attending enterprises allowed me to achieve my goals and overcome the frustration of isolation. It was the first time I was able to connect with like-minded people of a similar age. Looking into the mirror 2 years on, Enterprisers has given me more motivation, energy, drive and passion than one person could ever need to be successful. Thank you.

## 8.5 Jessamy Kelly Juo Ltd — Participant and Entrepreneur

I heard about Enterprisers through the University of Sunderland — it was a call out for graduate/post-graduate students to attend a funded business programme. I was interested in considering self-employment as I had previously only worked in industry and as a PhD Student. I wanted to see if there were connections between my emerging research/work and what might be the start of an innovative business idea or potential venture. Also having worked in industry I was aware of how things can be run sometimes badly when you work for someone else and you don't have the control/authority to make changes.

I was expecting perhaps some general business advise and networking. I definitely got more than I expected, the varied sessions and tasks were really a fantastic way to get an idea of what business is about and different ways that it can be approached. I have been on other business courses since and none were as interesting or fun as Enterprisers.

The programme was really engaging and it was great to see different characters come out of the group. It was almost as if you could see people's confidence and potential growing as the week passed. I am usually a pretty confident person but I definitely felt my confidence grow. Barriers were quickly broken down and inhibitions disappeared. I felt it was a very open and relaxed atmosphere — ideal for fostering new ideas and developing new skills! It was also a great experience to work within the dynamic of a diverse group — reacting as an individual and a group to different challenges and tasks.

When my business partner and I started planning the business we broke it down into different structures and time scales using post-its which we then used to create a business blueprint: this was definitely something that I brought away from the programme with me.

I was also inspired by the enterprisers experience in that there are so many diverse people — contacts/networks that you can work with. And the message that you don't need to be an expert in everything. Since starting up the business I have found that it is best to surround the business with good people that can help to sustain it. We now work with a real mix of people: photographers, web hosts, designers, sales agents, suppliers, etc., to get our business right. I think a lesson I learnt early on was that it's all about people and communicating with them to get things to work and to sustain this process if you don't maintain this things go wrong. I feel this was definitely an underlying message from Enterprisers.

Professor Max Robinson gave us some business, through the Blueprint Business Planning Competition. I have also stayed in touch with a few of the alumni who have been interested in my work and are keen to hear my news about the business.

Hot off the press as the book was being written:

> "Good news! We have just celebrated our 3rd year in business, enterprisers definitely got my ideas going and gave me the motivation to take them forwards to form a creative glass design business — Juo Ltd with fellow designer Joanne Mitchell. We are based at the National Glass Centre, in Sunderland and specialise in the design and production of high quality fused art glass wall panels for modern interiors. We have worked with some fantastic clients including Newcastle Building Society, NHS Trust, UKTI, Great North Run, Tekla, NOF Energy and Finance Tree. It has been great to be a part of enterprisers and it is always a privilege to come back and talk about the business to new recruits!

## 8.6 Chris Ireland — Participant and Ambassador in the Public Sector

I haven't started a business yet, but Enterprisers certainly gave me the confidence to do anything, and lasting friendships. I ran a statewide business competition in Queensland, Australia, and now work on the Asia Pacific Cities Summit in the International Relations Unit for the Lord Mayor of Brisbane's Administration Office. I'd love to see Enterprisers back in Queensland, Australia.

## 8.7 Matias Piipari — Participant and Entrepreneur

There were a few important moments in Enterprisers that sort of connected some pieces together in my head. First was realising that I seem to actually have some skills in working with people I hadn't really thought of. A few intense days of working together with the sort of enthusiastic and lively people who were present there can be a really positive experience for a boring academic.

I'd say the biggest thing that has helped me in actually pushing our real finished products through development is simply being more aware of the role I take in a team and adapting that depending on who else is working with me and what we actually want to accomplish. Sounds really vague and obvious, I know, but this is honestly something I only thought of after Enterprisers. This sort of skill is especially important given that the 5 people who are now part of our development team are all in different parts of Europe physically (me in United Kingdom, three in Finland, my business partner in Spain) and motivated by rather different types of things — none of us has put large sums of money into the company and we all spend time when we could be sleeping coding away software projects. Somehow motivation has to be kept up.

Making short pitches I remember also being nice because it's such a different style of presentation than what PhD students like us get used to.

Feedback from the facilitators was also very useful and I had very good conversations about the product idea I had at the time which got developed into an open source software package called Mindwiki (http://www.mindwiki.net/) through a student-run development team in University of Tampere, Finland later that year. This project got started through me realising soon after Enterprisers that I know people who organise a software development project in University of Tampere — I acted as a client who'd ordered the development of my idea for the course, and 9 students worked on the application for approximately 200 man hours each.

Inspired by Enterprisers, I attended another short entrepreneur course. And combining this course with what I had taken away from

Enterprisers, I built up some contacts and have since started an iPhone development company called Pear computing on the side of my studies. This I run with a colleague. We have managed to get a few clients for a small application development project and the results of our first project are on the iTunes app Store. It is a picture dictionary application called "Point Don't Shout. (http://www.pointdontshout.com).

Enterprisers was a great experience and made me think for the first time that maybe I could actually become an entrepreneur and about the types of skills and experiences I should gather during the remainder of my graduate studies to get started as one.

I also started thinking during Enterprisers about the contacts I have. Getting started with a small part-time business on the side of studying for a PhD has required lots of people from mine and my business partner's network ranging from software developers (there were two other people I know from back home in Finland now working for us for different projects), a game designer/journalist who's written pieces about us to *NY Times* website, to a lawyer and an accountant.

## 8.8 James Duggan — Participant and Social Entrepreneur

After attending Enterprisers I pottered around with a couple of ideas that failed to get going but it got me talking to people and this gave me a sense that I could actually do something, and here are some personal milestones.

In the education department at Manchester, there is an NGO that disseminates information on inclusive education in developing countries. To help them cope with the changing fundraising context as a result of the credit crunch I initiated and part-managed a project to establish a social enterprise consultancy to help bring in revenue for the charitable side of the organisation.

I've developed a project to launch a cooperative in a secondary school in a food desert community in east Manchester this September. A food desert community is an area where the residents don't have ready access to affordable fresh food and so live of an expensive and unhealthy diet of fast food and ready meals. Through the cooperative the pupils will sell food to the community while the school will stage cooking classes in the community to increase (the project is based on the assumption that no one is selling fresh food because no one is buying it because people have lost the skills to cook food from fresh ingredients.) The idea of the project is to provide school children with an incentive to promote healthier lifestyles in their local community, similar to peer-to-peer marketing used by toy manufacturers. The project will hopefully teach the school children about business and enterprise, about food, about healthy lifestyles and build relationships between the school and the community.

In trying to start a social enterprise at university, I became aware of how bad my university is at utilising the vast resources available to make a substantive and efficient contribution to the city's poorer communities. For social enterprise week, I am organising a mini-conference to explain what social enterprise is and showcase the number of social enterprises in the university and the local community. I am also working with the post-graduate and post-doctoral training departments to run interdisciplinary workshops where researchers can meet councillors and academics, etc., to learn about contemporary problems in the city and develop project solutions that can be staffed and implemented by Manchester university students. In the long term, I am looking to create a community of social entrepreneurs in the university.

I thought the main benefit from attending the Enterprisers course was getting to meet all the impressive speakers, facilitators and participants. I'm not from an elite university and I felt quite privileged to share the experience with so many people who have achieved so much. When I came back from enterprises, I was markedly different. (Someone joked that I'd joined a cult.) Since going on the course I got a sense of confidence and urgency and after a couple of false starts I've created a network through which I can make things happen.

## 8.9 David Owen

Over the past two years I have embarked on the Enterprisers journey three times, twice of which as a facilitator, and continue to be inspired and energised by the intensive nature of the course. Unlike most professional and academic courses which make you sit at a desk and recite processes and methodologies at you, Enterprisers is largely about personal ambitions and what you can offer to the enterprising world, focussing on personal reflection throughout and delivering a unique journey to each delegate. The lead facilitators come from academic and practical background in the field affording them a wide range of case studies, examples and an abundance of amusing anecdotes! In a world of professional courses and accreditations Enterprisers is a real breath of fresh air, and I wouldn't hesitate to recommend it to anyone.

## 8.10 University of Sussex — Capturing Institutional Impact

University of Sussex, is a world leading teaching and research institution. In the 2008 Times Higher Education University World Rankings, Sussex was ranked in the top 20 in the United Kingdom, the top 50 in Europe and the top 150 worldwide. Sussex has over 11,000 students from over 120 countries. Sussex has developed a reputation for innovation and inspiration, and attracts leading thinkers and researchers. Sussex have counted three Nobel Prize winners, 13 Fellows of the Royal Society, six Fellows of the British Academy and a winner of the prestigious Crafoord Prize on our faculty. As much as 90% of Sussex academics' research has international impact.

The University's Regional Development Office (RDO) is the main contact point for business, public sector and other organisations wishing to engage with the university. The team provides specialist advice and access to university expertise. The RDO is also responsible for developing enterprise and entrepreneurship activity for students across the university and managing knowledge transfer partnerships.

The University of Sussex played host to two of the early Enterprisers, sponsored by the South East England Development Agency (SEEDA), a regional body that took up the programme with full energy to bring about a cohesive provision of entrepreneurship education among the 27 higher educational institutions in the region.

Before Enterprisers was hosted at University of Sussex there was no visible or viable set of programmes, but there was an office, part of the outreach and technology transfer activity. The staff was keen to engage in providing entrepreneurship education across the University, mainly because there was no Business School at Sussex. Enterprisers, gave the team at Sussex an excellent opportunity to showcase entrepreneurship education, engage the senior faculty and administrators of the university and bring a project to the students to gauge reaction and to build on the programme if things went well.

The Sussex team, from the perspective of working as collaborators for Enterprisers, are a superbly open-minded group, who want to make a difference to the students and the overall culture of the institution. So, the team responded to the design, training, content and development of Enterprisers. They worked "full-on" to make Enterprisers a success on both occasions.

The key impact was that the programme was "brought" to Sussex, showcased to senior colleagues and created a momentum from which a number of initiatives, projects and activities have been launched. At a personal level too, it demonstrated to the individuals in the team that such a programme could be delivered, that students responded well to it and through the support of sponsors, the programme could also more than breakeven.

The Sussex team also approached one of their corporate partners, American Express (Amex) with whom they run a Masters programme and persuaded them to send some of the trainees to the programme. This too has become a long-term gain for Sussex, Enterprisers and the individuals in the company.

In summary the main impacts have been as follows:

- Personal development for the team at Sussex and for the participants who have been supported on Enterprisers.

- New social networks have been created, nurtured and developed.
- Enterprisers are acted as a catalyst for enterprise activity. Please see Table 8.1 below for the list of activities.
- Enterprise provision grown hugely since 2005. In total, the number of students taking part has grown from zero to over 600 per year.
- The Pro Vice Chancellor has now included Entrepreneurship education into the University as a 10-year strategy.

"Create a culture of enterprise and innovation across the University, embedded in our core educational and research activities" addition to the courses that have been developed, The University of Sussex has also developed collaborations on three levels as follows:

### 8.10.1 *Collaborations*

As a result of Enterprisers, the team at Sussex made new contacts and connections on national, regional and international levels. This has enabled the team to generate profile for Sussex, create new projects for its students and further novel interactions, all of which add to the enhanced climate for entrepreneurship promotion and development at the University (Table 8.2).

Sussex and the National Council for Graduate Entrepreneurship (NCGE) forged their relationship after the NCGE's Director for Flying Start Programmes facilitated at the 2005 SEEDA funded Enterprisers programme at Sussex. Once the relationship was established many opportunities were created. Many Sussex students have attended programmes and workshops run by the NCGE, such as Flying Start. Sussex was also introduced to the prestigious Kauffman Entrepreneurship Fellows scheme in 2007, run by the NCGE. Sussex was lucky enough to have 2 of their aspiring entrepreneurial students win scholarships and spent 6 months in the United States developing their business ideas.

Enterprisers also acted as a launching board for Sussex and its involvement with both Higher Education Entrepreneurship Group (HEEG) and Enterprise Educators United Kingdom (EEUK). HEEG and EEUK aim to increase the capacities and capabilities of higher

**Table 8.1.** Summary of the Diversity and Extent of Enterprise Activity at University of Sussex — Post Enterprisers

| Enterprise activities at sussex | Sussex level | Regional level | National level | International level | Description | Open to: |
|---|---|---|---|---|---|---|
| Enterprise Thursdays | | | | | Speaker events featuring entrepreneurs, then networking | Businesses, staff and students |
| Enter-prize annual ideas competition comprising 3 stages | | Make a difference Ideas Comp | Enterprise educators UK "Winners" Comp | | Annual ideas competition comprising 3 stages. Students encouraged to apply for external competitions | PG and UG students Business judges required |
| Junior Research Associates (JRA's) workshops | | | | | Enterprise activities provided as part of JRA programme | UG 2nd-year business judges required |
| Xing Business Strategy game (licensed to UoS) | Interschool competition | | National competition | | Workshops and in-house competition, followed by national competition | UG and PG business judges required |

*(Continued)*

**Table 8.1.** (*Continued*)

| Enterprise activities at sussex | Sussex level | Regional level | National level | International level | Description | Open to: |
|---|---|---|---|---|---|---|
| Students in free Enterprise (SIFE) | | Regional competition | National competition | Links with SIFE teams across the world | Global not-for-profit org, with national arm, down to student society level. | UG students Business advisors sought |
| PG creativity café workshop | | | | | 1 day event for PGs, in InQbate Enterprise skills development | Postgraduates |
| NCGE — Flying start programme | | | | | National org, providing research and development programmes | UG, PG, graduates, staff |
| SEEDA/HEEG | | | | | Regional funding/ enterprise educators network | Academic and professional staff |
| Enterprisers undergraduate | | | | | Cambridge and MIT residential programme | UG students |

(*Continued*)

Table 8.1.  (*Continued*)

| Enterprise activities at sussex | Sussex level | Regional level | National level | International level | Description | Open to: |
|---|---|---|---|---|---|---|
| Enterprisers postgraduate | | | | | As above | PG students (often RC funded) |
| Commercialise | | | | | Training and mentoring for those wishing to start a business | UG, PG, staff, and graduates |
| Global enterprise week | | | Make your mark | | Annual campaign. Extra activities and publicity | Businesses, staff and students |
| CDEC jobs/ enterprise fund | | | | | Free advertising for businesses, with opportunities for students and graduates | Fund for UG/PG student projects |
| LINKS European 9 × French 3 × Belgian Universities | | | | | European projects with funding for collaborative enterprise projects | Varies: UG/ PG/Staff/ businesses |

**Table 8.2.** Collaborations Generated by University of Sussex through New Networks from Enterprisers

| International | National | Regional |
|---|---|---|
| Kauffman Foundation, Kansas | NCGE | HEEG |
| Idèlab, Sweden | Enterprisers Educators UK | SEEDA |
| AMEX | SIFE UK | Commercialise |

education to develop more enterprising students and more graduate business start-ups through up-skilling staff and sharing best practice. Since being introduced to many HEEG and EEUK members who were also involved in Enterprisers programmes, Sussex are regular attendees of their best practise sharing events and workshops, and contributes regularly to the contents of the events. The friendly relationships built up during the Enterprisers programmes, and reinforced through contact at EEUK and HEEG workshops has meant that enterprise educators can regularly pick up the phone to one another and share best practise on an informal basis. For example, a past Enterprisers facilitator on the SEEDA-funded Enterprisers programme recently contacted a member of staff at Sussex to ask how they manage their enterprise student representative team so that they could take tips and take it back to their institution of Chichester University.

On 21st June 2007, Sussex hosted a conference on Creativity in Teaching and Learning, in partnership with HEEG and LINKS. The conference was attended by academics from institutions all over the United Kingdom, as well as academics and educators from 9 French Universities. The event included active and lively discussions on creativity in teaching and learning, as well as the opportunity to discover examples of creative approaches to teaching and learning from international institutions. Many new networks and relationships were formed at the event itself.

Following a knowledge exchange visit from Eskistuna, Sweden, colleagues from the University of Mälardalens' Idélab centre were interested in learning about the Enterprisers programme and keen to share their creativity and team-building techniques as well as their system of integrating university and science park support for student and graduate business ideas. Further involvement with creativity events at Sussex has stemmed from this collaboration.

SEEDA continue to work together with Sussex on many aspects of the entrepreneurial activity.

CommercialiSE is a partnership of 11 universities with part funding from SEEDA, and it offers early stage funding and business fellows training. Since 2007 when Sussex began being involved in CommercialiSE, around 17 staff, students and alumni have been through the course and developed their business ideas.

Relationships between facilitators from Sussex and their co-facilitators on Enterprisers programmes has always bred new opportunity. It was having heard about SIFE UK from other enterprise educators at different institutions that Sussex decided to get involved in 2007. SIFE is a global not-for-profit organisation aimed at university students from all academic disciplines, who are encouraged to establish teams and develop projects that create economic opportunity for others. Since Sussex student Luke Fletcher decided to establish SIFE Sussex (Luke was also employed by the University of Sussex in 2006 to help with the administration of many entrepreneurial activities at the University) in 2007 it has grown from strength to strength. SIFE Sussex now has over 20 active members working on two projects; one in a community in Malawi, and one in local schools in Sussex.

Sussex was very much involved in both Australian Enterprisers programmes in 2007 and 2008, having both facilitators and students from Sussex attend the programmes. Once again new links and relationships were formed, this time internationally. Richard Thorning, Director of Entrepreneurship & Executive Education at Curtin Business School, who was also a facilitator on the Australian programme has recently been on a visit to the University of Sussex. As well as catching up with his co-facilitator, he also met academics from Sussex and the Director of Sussex's Innovation Centre to share knowledge and discuss entrepreneurial activities at the others' institution.

## 8.10.2 *Creating an Enterprising Culture at the University*

The team at Sussex also bought into the fact that enterprise education was more than business skills. It embodies, risk taking, creativity, idea generation, positive attitudes, and the social and business skills to enable new ideas, ventures and projects to happen. It also links to future employability skills, as well as the ability to seek self-employment or create new ventures. Many of the tools used on Enterprisers have stimulated and inspired the Sussex team into creating activities, events and projects that bring about a greater sense of enterprise.

---

XING: University of
Sussex Competition

Over the last 2 years we have held "in-house" Xing competitions to put together a Sussex Xing team to represent our university at the Regional and National Flux finals. XING (formerly known as YOMP) is an interactive strategy game whereby a small team of students go through the thought and decision processes and stages of setting up a new venture. It doesn't matter if you want to set up your own business or not — it's about thinking creatively, being entrepreneurial and working within a team.

---

(*Continued*)

*(Continued)*

FLUX: Regional
   and National
   XING Competitions

In both 2008 and 2009 Sussex have
   entered teams into the FLUX finals in
   Plymouth where our teams have
   competed against other XING teams
   from universities all over the
   country. FLUX is a valuable
   experience for students increasing
   their confidence in presenting
   and networking whilst encouraging
   teamworking and creative thinking;
   it also makes a valuable addition
   to their CV.

A quote from one of the 2008 Sussex
   XING team members:

> *"I strongly believe that everyone should
> give Flux a chance no matter what
> degree they are currently pursuing, as
> this competition is not about applying
> managerial theoretical aspects but
> about meeting new people and
> discovering things about yourself
> you had no idea you were capable
> of doing." Carmen Gheoldus,
> University of Sussex Xing 08 Team
> Member.*

*(Continued)*

---

(*Continued*)

---

Enterprise Thursdays

Enterprise Thursdays were inspired by
Cambridge University's series of
Enterprise Tuesdays. The evening
events begin with a talk by an
inspirational person from the world
of business, charity or social enterprise.
Each Enterprise Thursday concentrates
upon a particular theme, and the
audience is encouraged to ask questions
throughout, to make the event as
interactive as possible. The talk is
followed by the chance to network
and get to know the other students,
and staff, and the chance to talk to the
speaker on a more informal level.

Enterprise Thursdays are open to all and
are attended not only by students
but also by staff, members of the local
business community, alumni and
academics creating a diverse audience
and opening  lines of communication
on an informal level between the
university and local businesses.
Through Enterprise Thursdays we
have created links with prestigious
organisations such as the Institute

---

(*Continued*)

*(Continued)*

---

of Directors and Rotary Club,
and strengthened and developed
links with local organisations such as
Wired Sussex and The Werks.

Students in Free
Enterprise (SIFE)

SIFE Sussex is a University of Sussex
  society affiliated to the global,
  non-profit organisation, (SIFE). SIFE
  Sussex is a relatively new organisation
  that was established by the first SIFE
  Sussex president, Luke Fletcher, in
  2007 with the help and encouragement
  of the Regional Development Office.
  SIFE offers students the opportunity
  to make positive differences in their
  local community and also internationally,
  whilst gaining experience, skills, and
  entrepreneurial thinking to aid them in
  their future lives. Each university team
  sets up, and implements sustainable
  projects aimed at specific community
  groups which are designed to "Help
  people help themselves" by transferring
  skills, knowledge and support to enable
  particular groups to succeed in the
  future. In both 2008 and 2009 the
  SIFE Sussex team competed in

---

*(Continued)*

*(Continued)*

---

the SIFE National Competition and received excellent comments and feedback from the judges.

Students in Free
Enterprise (SIFE)

The Regional Development Office offer support and guidance to the SIFE Sussex team. The Student Enterprise Team act as SIFE Team advisors and meet regularly with the SIFE Sussex President and the project leaders to offer advice on fundraising, feedback on presentations and give general guidance. The Regional Development Office also provide practical support allowing the SIFE Sussex team access to our meeting rooms and equipment.
The SIFE Sussex Team has two voluntary projects, one local and one overseas. Both of these projects aim to educate underprivileged or underachieving young people to become more entrepreneurial, teaching them basic life and business skills. The SIFE Sussex Team regularly holds fundraising

---

*(Continued)*

*(Continued)*

---

events for these two projects including cake
sales and book sales. In addition to these
activities they have also made presentations
to the local Rotary Club and received
donations from them. Over the last year
SIFE Sussex have raised thousands of
pounds to support their two projects.

---

### 8.10.3  *Adoption of Tools from Enterprisers for Use at Sussex*

The tools are used incrementally. First comes "Creativity Cafe" based on World Cafe — easily available on the web, which is used for the generation of creativity, new ideas, inspiring actions and new ventures. The outputs of the creativity session are fed into Ketso — used to help students identify resources and actions needed to start to shape the idea onto reality. Finally the resources are identified and the actions required are mapped out using Xing, which further combines business-planning tools. All the three activities are facilitated and can lead to very practical learning about oneself and about how to generate ideas and how to take them forward. In addition students learn that the process is not linear, that there is much tacit knowledge required and open conversations are most helpful in moving ideas forward.

The three activities can either be linked as a set or can be used individually, as Sussex has done in taking part in Xing national competitions to help students understand strategy, planning and competition in business. Creativity cafe has been a stimulant for Sussex to create bespoke workshops for post-graduate researchers which we held on campus in InQbate, a Centre of Excellence in Teaching and Learning in Creativity.

We have grown in confidence and in 2008 implemented a completely new activity, Enter-priZe, the first ideas competition at the University of Sussex. Enter-priZe was launched in 2008 and following a positive response will become an annual event. We encouraged not only business ideas but also innovative product ideas, social enterprise ideas and service ideas. In our first year, we received over 80 entries across the two different stages of the competition. The judges for the final two stages were made up of members of faculty, student union and also local entrepreneurs who were all very impressed at the high standard of the entries the students had submitted.

## Creativity Café Workshop

Unleash your creative side and develop entrepreneurial skills in a 1 day Workshop for Postgraduates

**Learn how to :**

. Generate ideas
. Collaborate effectively
. Practise presenting
. Work in a team

Wednesday 10th June
10am—4pm
Lunch included

To register, please email sp2@sussex.ac.uk with your name, department and year

## 8.11  Newcastle University

Newcastle's story is one of how Enterprisers had an impact at an individual level and how that has empowered, informed and steered institutional approaches and developments inside and outside of the curriculum as well as at a strategic level.

One of the biggest problems about enterprise education and entrepreneurial development is that educators and stakeholders that are new to it find it hard to leave their pre-conceived definitions about the terms to one side to focus on the processes and outcomes of the learner/participant... and these are the educators! Imagine the difficulty the students and graduates have. The truth that Enterprisers helped us to discover is that definitions have their place in the mechanisms that make (or at least try to make) institutions and programmes work, but until you have engaged with the process and jumped into the deep end of learning, knowledge and skills, in a supportive environment, you be limited by those definitions. Enterprisers, and learning by doing in general, allows educators and learners to see through those limits and benefit from an implicit understanding that motivates and raises aspirations.

In many ways this was confirmation rather than revelation, but exploitation of the benefits was to be enhanced significantly by an initial encounter with Enterprisers in its early years. In the late 1990s, early nought-ies, Newcastle University's Careers Service had a team dedicated to the understanding of work-related learning, employability and the support of academic staff embedding the above. From a theoretical perspective and thanks to several effective curriculum development projects, there was a broad commitment to the learning by doing approach to student development.

Some of these curriculum development projects had been funded by the North East Centre for Scientific Enterprise (NECSE), (the Science Enterprise Challenge Centre for the North East of England Universities). Coupled with drivers such as the Regional Economic Strategy, NECSE's mission together with the University's exploration of self-employment in a career context began to inspire an increasingly robust institutional focus on enterprise and entrepreneurship.

NECSE's Education Manager at the time, academic entrepreneur Prof Max Robinson, was both passionate and enchanted by the challenge that the curriculum proposed to the development of enterprise and was always interested in how Newcastle was experimenting inside and outside of the curriculum.

You have to know Prof Robinson to understand that when he recommends something, it is highly likely to be something that is worth investigating, as it was when he suggested that someone from the Careers Service should travel half-an-hour south from Newcastle to see a new Cambridge — MIT Institute residential course in action at Durham University. And so began Newcastle's fascination with Connections, soon to become Enterprisers.

A year later Newcastle University sent some students and a facilitator back to Durham to get under the skin of Enterprisers. At the end of the four days everyone involved, including the member of staff facilitating knew how to look beyond words and work with the enterprising spirit and entrepreneurial intentions that can exist in anyone prepared to try. Suddenly the purpose of enterprise education was clearer, the process of entrepreneurial development was more coherent and most importantly the aim was more tangible. The facilitator then, an enterprise development officer from Newcastle University, was able to champion the Enterprisers approach and, as a consequence of the role, affect the development of the Careers Service and its offering over the subsequent years, using skills and approaches that the course itself had unleashed and a sense of self-efficacy that the course had emboldened.

As a result of this work, the University now considers enterprise as a core aspect of a Newcastle graduate. Since its inclusion in the university's new Graduate Skills Framework, all taught programmes at Newcastle University have been embedding it along with elements such as business-planning skills and market awareness. Fuelled in part with the evidence from Enterprisers it was possible to argue that enterprise should be mainstreamed across all of the activities of the Careers Service demonstrating that a resourceful, opportunistic and ethically aware approach finding a job was considered effective. The Entrepreneurial Development Unit (EDU) within the Careers Service supports those students and graduates who choose to apply their enterprise to their own venture.

The conceptual framework around which the EDU and its services are built, is underpinned by the Enterprisers notion of starting with the values and aspirations of the individual, providing them with practical tools and techniques to explore their ideas, offering them networks of experts to help with the technicalities of creating a new venture, whilst building an empowering environment and set of relationships throughout the process. This is summarised by the EDU's statement of purpose:

*Working in partnership with University colleagues, the business support community and national and regional policy makers to help students, graduates and researchers turn entrepreneurial ideas into action.*

The EDU's approach, and that of its preceding units, is now so aligned to the Enterprisers 'way' that new members of staff are volunteered as facilitators on Enterprisers courses as part of their orientation. This is particularly effective with regards to the bits of being a "pracademic" enterprise animateur that can't be written and must be experienced. The long relationship with Enterprisers and the experience of participating in various versions (including some that Newcastle University has funded), has facilitated the use of tools and techniques developed and incubated by Enterprisers to be used. EDU delivers eight enterprise and entrepreneurship modules at Newcastle and every one will use tools such as XING or Ketso or World Café to help provide practical opportunities for entrepreneurial learning. The EDU also propagates the use of these tools amongst other educators on campus and are involved in research projects to try to get closer to the secrets of success.

The use of common tools has a very tangible impact of Newcastle University's involvement with Enterprisers, but there are a few key ingredients that the EDU try to apply to all of its interventions with its clients, that have been collected as the staff and student experience of Enterprisers deepens:

- Stimulating characters — Involving entrepreneurs and interesting people in education not only introduces someone with a relevant story but also provides a novel feature of the educational experience that stimulates the participants to enquire and learn more. Enterprisers, thanks to its growing networks, has always been able to pull in fascinating people. At Newcastle University we nurture our networks so that the same kind of interesting people with a novelty about them can enrich our curriculum.

- Diverse teams — Enterprisers traditionally recruits participants from a wide range of backgrounds and origins. This is most potently demonstrated with the "Map of the World" creativity exercise. The greater the number of differences such as culture, degree discipline, age and aspiration within a team of participants, the greater the creativity that is possible, but also the more beneficial the journey. The greater the number of differences between members of task teams, the further they have to go to find a common connection to start growing together. In the post-graduate training at Newcastle teams are constructed to exploit differences in technical knowledge so that they can communicate more openly (limited jargon can be understood) and address problems with innovative solutions.

- Intense experiences — Being confined to one place to live, learn and socialise on Enterprisers can be very challenging to people. But this intensity is observed as a key driver for participants to address their reservations and begin connecting and growing with each other. It is considered as one of the key contributors to the development of self-efficacy. Participants have to determine who they are and what they have to offer very quickly to play their part in the teams and benefit from the course. The tight deadline on tasks also means that many of the barriers to teamwork are pushed to one side for the benefit of all. These personally "high stakes" situations are replicated in Newcastle University module exercises and in some post-graduate training courses, which are not yet residential, but are intense in other ways.

- Supportive environment — There is no doubt that the journey the participant embarks upon when joining Enterprisers would not be as effective was it not for the professionalism of the facilitators.

Their immediate challenge is to make everyone feel welcome and create the safe and trustworthy environment in which to discuss sensitive issues and personal aspirations in front of strangers. This support grows to be reinforced by the team members themselves allowing the facilitators to start to empower individuals. At Newcastle University the relationship with clients is based on the notion that, "if a facilitator can demonstrate that they believe the client can do something, the client will at the very least try to succeed with it". It very often takes this "faith" in the enterprising spirit to encourage it to surface in an individual. When this happens in a safe surrounding, anything is possible.

## 8.12  The Ah Ha Moments — What Shai and Neal have Learned after Many Experiments

After repeatedly facilitating on enterprisers, pulling together a curriculum, team, speakers and content, as well as attracting sponsors and students, what are we as leaders of enterprisers able to reflect on? Each programme ideally runs on a critical mass of about 60 participants and 16+ facilitators. This critical mass of participants can create a vibrant environment and a self-fuelling source of energy, tacit knowledge and connections.

The programme needs to be residential — as it just takes time to get to know people and the evening informal sessions are just as important as the formal events during the day. Sometimes people just do not "get it" and often go to their rooms after the formal sessions and the dinner. They need to be encouraged to "hang around" to pick up small talk and random discussions as all this is part of building a social ecosystem that can be supportive in the future.

Diversity — in many different ways — disciplines, institutional participation, nationalities and even a somewhat wide range of ages can be hugely beneficial. The programme also needs to get a good balance in terms of gender participation.

Although we have seen great benefits in age range participation — we have found the cocktail of more senior people from industry participating in the programme has not been a huge success. The main reason is that many of them receive "training" in terms of social skills and many of the tools used on Enterprisers will feel familiar to them. What we have found is for those people who come with a totally open mind and even if they have benefited from the past training take away the intended benefits of the programme. In the case that organisers want to include people from companies, it is best to recruit those who are in the more junior roles and can benefit from the programme.

Unlocking creativity — needs a tight — loose format of event management. On the one hand organisers need to have quite a tight control over the pace, direction and activities, but within Enterprisers there needs to be a huge amount of flexibility. The key to this tight — loose format is that the lead facilitators and administration team, facilitators and venue management are all kept informed and agree on the detail.

The radical design we instigated at the very start of the experiment can now best be summarised as a programme that combines personal self awareness, with business know-how and social skill building as the cornerstones to enabling entrepreneurial learning. This insight is now quite pervasive in our other programmes in sustainable ways.

We have seen subtle blends of interaction among participants which tells us that Enterprisers may be used for more than the development of individual self-efficacy — it could be used for wider social change. The internal activities are quite powerful in unleashing creativity, so when you think about how we bring talented people from everywhere, one starts to think that the activities could be for tangible outputs as well as for personal development of individuals. We need to make a strong experiment in this direction to be fully convinced, because it would change the complexion of the programme.

We trained trainers in real time! One of the most underrated outcomes of the programme — is that we have been training trainers in real time and the individuals who have been working with us on this — always in a voluntary capacity have taken lessons back into their own programmes, universities and even into companies to instil some of the spirit, tools and detail of the programme to make changes. We have had the contributions from Sussex and Newcastle Universities to illustrate this point, but anecdotally we are aware that there are many other such positive stories to tell. The real story is that while we may have trained over a 1000 graduates, the total is probably 10 times that number through the inspired application of the tools by our facilitators — whom we salute! We hope this book inspires many more to get out there and continue to unlock the enterprisers inside their own communities.

## Endnotes

1. Lead facilitators and facilitators participated in a "Train-the-trainer" event developed by Ashridge Consulting. Hartmut Stuelten presented this model of modes of interaction during that training and we continue to include it as part of our facilitator training.
2. John Heron presented his six styles of managing and leading in his 1975 work *Helping the Client*. We find the styles useful in talking about different facilitation techniques.
3. B. Tuckman and M. Jensen discussed their "Stages of Small Group Development" in *Group and Organisational Studies* 2: 419–427 (1977). The five stages continue to be explored in courses looking at stages of group development.